CULTIVATE

*a youth worker's guide
to establishing
healthy relationships*

MATT WILKS

bare
foot
MINISTRIES®

Copyright 2011 by Barefoot Ministries®

ISBN 978-0-8341-5060-7

Printed in the United States of America

Editor: Audra C. Marvin
Cover Design: Arthur Cherry

Library of Congress Cataloging-in-Publication Data: 2011932947

10 9 8 7 6 5 4 3 2 1

To the many people who have believed in me and my call
and have let me lead you, thank you.

To Grandpa Bruce, who reminds me every time I see him
that he is proud of me because I am in love with Jesus.

To my parents, who believed in me and sacrificed
in ways beyond what was needed, thank you.

To Maris and Macauleigh, who remind me every day
that the greatest call of my life is to be a pastor.
I love you both more than words can express.

To Michelle, your sacrifices for me and our daughters are incredible.
You are even more beautiful than you were when we married
many years ago. If I had known then what I know now,
I would easily have made the choice again to marry you.

To God the Father, I love you and am so thrilled
to be in this adventure with you.
I long for the day when I can
"be still and know that you are God."

CONTENTS

FOREWORD

By Marv Penner

After more than four decades of in-the-trenches youth ministry and almost thirty years of training youth workers in colleges and seminaries around the world, I think I've learned a thing or two about what places men and women for in effective positions to pursue their callings. But sadly, I've also seen what has caused more than a few of them to fail miserably.

I've watched straight-A students, who wrote brilliantly crafted term papers and research projects with thoughtful thesis statements and a hundred footnotes, crash and burn in their first year or two in the trenches. I've seen my share of gifted and skilled ministry practitioners, who could fire off a youth talk that brought kids to their knees and plan outreach events that filled the parking lot, flounder and fail in spite of their incredible programming proficiency. A casual observer might wonder how someone with such an apparent depth of understanding or well-developed skill set could experience anything but success. Was there something missing? Apparently the answer is yes.

Is it possible that there's more to long-term ministry effectiveness than technical understanding or brilliant program execution? Is there a third factor, not as easily defined and perhaps not as easily measured that is even more fundamentally important than the two aforementioned attributes? There certainly is! It's the piece a lot of starting youth workers say they didn't learn in the classroom at college or seminary. It's the component that can't be evaluated very well on a pop quiz. Its absence or presence can even be missed in a job interview if it's not being specifically targeted. It's the part that sometimes feels invisible and elusive—and it's the topic of this book.

It's been said that long-term effectiveness in ministry is based on the full engagement of head, hands, and heart.

The head refers to the knowledge base, theoretical foundations, or basic content upon which the practices of youth ministry are built. It's a constantly evolving and expanding body of truth that becomes the starting point for much of what is done to achieve appropriate ministry outcomes. And it's important for every serious youth worker to master. It consists of things like biblical literacy, theological truth, theories of adolescent development and family systems, models of leadership, denominational distinctives, cultural trends, and a whack of other knowledge without which it's difficult to move forward confidently.

The good news is that this knowledge base is becoming easier than ever to access. Thousands of books and the global storehouse of electronic information put mountains of great material at the fingertips of motivated students. Formal education has made a science out of delivering content well. The church has traditionally done a great job of delivering the *what* of ministry.

But there's also the matter of the *how*, and here's where the hands become the metaphor. We're talking about ministry methodology (or praxis, if you need a fancy word for it.) It's all about competence, and it comes down to the basic skills that are required to be able to do the tasks of ministry: how to structure a great lesson or talk; how to ask good questions when working with hurting teens or their families; how to plan and balance a budget; how to edit video; how to deliver an illustration well; how to teach a group a new game; how to drive a fifteen-passenger van; how to make s'mores; how to lead worship; how to plan a good retreat. The list can seem endless, but it actually matters. When a church or ministry organization hires someone, it's appropriate for them to assume that the individual will be able to pull it off—and pull it off well!

In recent years, many of our best training programs have adapted their training strategies based on the understanding that ministry skills are best learned in a well-supervised internship or in a mentored apprenticeship where a rookie receives constructive evaluation and constant feedback. Ministry veterans and organizational leaders collaborate to establish best practices, and hands-on training programs roll out new approaches. We're doing a pretty good job of teaching people the *how*.

But what about that crucial third component—the heart? The heart deals with the *who*. It is by far the most subjective of the three but undoubtedly the most critical component in determining the long-term outcome of one's ministry journey. Content is mastered through thoughtful reading, classroom engagement, and good conversation where conflicting ideas are processed. Competence is acquired through practice, trial and error, and thoughtful evaluation and feedback. Character, however, must be *cultivated*. It's a matter of relational maturity, spiritual depth, personal discipline, and brutally honest self-awareness. It's about how a person responds to authority, resolves conflict, functions on a team, deals with criticism, serves others, and most importantly, how one lives out his or her personal relationship with God.

This is the heart of ministry and the single most significant component in an effective life. Unfortunately, there is no shortcut to achieving character. Content can be crammed, and competence can be faked, but character takes time and intentionality. It's hard work. And what makes it even harder is that it is often shaped in the context of our relationships.

Some people might say that character can't be learned, and in the strictest sense of the word, they might be right. But it can certainly be cultivated. This agricultural image is appropriate on so many levels. Cultivation brings order to places that are naturally wild, chaotic, and overgrown. Cultivation requires soil to be plowed and softened. And, of course, cultivation leads to fruitfulness. The Scripture is ripe with word pictures of grapevines, trees by the river, and grain fields ready for harvest. These are pictures of rich, productive lives, honoring the Creator and giving great joy to the individual.

You are holding in your hands a book about relationships in ministry. As you read, you will quickly come to understand that these relationships are the context in which your character will be cultivated (and of course the context in which your character will be lived out—for better or for worse).

Begin by carefully examining your relationship with God. The goal is to be fully conformed to the character of his Son. As Matt leads you on a reflective and responsive journey through the full range of relationships that mark your ministry journey, there will be numerous opportunities for you to allow (or resist) the penetrating, disrupting, often painful plow of God's Spirit to dig deeply into your heart.

As you think about your spouse, your kids, your boss, your volunteers, your ministry colleagues, and the many others introduced in this book, recognize that God is using them to bring order to your naturally chaotic relational world. See them as God's instruments to soften your heart and create in you a humble and teachable spirit. Embrace his desire to make your life more fruitful. The beauty of the process is that, as your character begins to align more closely with the character of Christ, you can move back into the very relationships that are shaping you and pour into them a life of gratitude, humility, and service.

You'll find some great content in this book, but please don't just read it with your head. There are also some really practical ideas that you can implement as new strategies or methods, but I urge you not to see it as merely a hands-on manual either. It's meant to tear up your heart a bit; to turn up some soil that may have been ignored or neglected for a while; to make your life and ministry more effective; to help you become a bit more like Jesus. There's no greater joy than that!

PREFACE

It was the summer of 1994 when a senior pastor from a Baptist church in Calgary asked me to consider joining his team while I was at a basketball camp. I would have never guessed as a young, twenty-two-year-old youth pastor that I would spend twelve years of my life there. Fresh with excitement and a Bible school degree, I set out on the journey of ministry. Two things ministry has taught me over all these years are the need to continually have a posture of learning and the value of relationships.

In many ways, I have had to learn about relationships the hard way. I have not valued people the way I should have, and I have, at times, simply misunderstood what people were trying to tell me. Even through all the mistakes, though, some of my fondest memories spring from the relationships I have built with fellow staff members, volunteers, and students.

This book has reminded me of each one of them, and writing this book has caused me to miss many of them dearly—people who have trusted in me with their hearts and have let me lead and share life with them. They truly have become the pastors to my family, and I deeply appreciate them.

This book is written as an instruction manual for you as you either enter into a church for the first time as a paid youth worker or as a key volunteer in a youth ministry setting. Some of you probably have been at this ministry role for longer than I have, and this book hopefully will serve as an encouragement to you as you stay faithful to your call. If you are an intern or a student, may this book help you stay away from the mistakes I made early in ministry.

I want to take you on a little journey before you even start to turn the pages of this book and introduce you to some people who made this ministry journey possible. And hopefully these introductions will give you some context for the stories that appear in the coming chapters.

My youth pastor, **Darrell**, who, in his own way, led a group of about thirty high school seniors to accomplish great things for God. At last count, there are twelve students from that grade who are currently in full-time ministry around the world. You did well, Darrell!

Frank, my college professor and dear friend, who took me along to everything during my first year of college so I could see that ministry is so much more than my little perspective.

My wife, **Michelle**, was the one who listened to God closely and made the decision to leave her family behind in Minnesota and encouraged me to take the job at Grace Baptist Church. Many times I questioned whether it had been the right decision, but I know it was definitely a God-orchestrated time.

Melanie, Darren, Sophie, and Lilly, my sister, brother-in-law, and nieces, who many times were forced into volunteering simply because they are family. Thank you for always being willing to chip in wherever was needed.

Pastor Kerber, who hired me and was my very first senior pastor. He taught me so much about how to value people and be their shepherd. God took him home early, maybe because he had completed what God wanted him to do here.

Pastor Jim, a senior pastor with whom I developed a deep ministry and relational friendship. His outlook, vision development, and ability to lead at a high level taught me so much about the business side of ministry.

The first students at Grace Baptist Church, who let me be their youth pastor. We watched videos most Wednesday nights simply because I wasn't prepared enough to teach. Many of you are the students about whom I am in awe of how God is using and has used you.

The **NABOB youth pastor network**, who let me as a young pastor be mentored by a group of godly guys. The way you challenged my ministry perceptions and philosophy is something that has shaped my life today.

Darian, a seventeen-year-old kid I met at a camp in Canada, who told me that God had called him to impact all of Canada. To my surprise (and shame for not trusting God), Darian was used by God to bring hundreds of youth pastors together in Canada.

The youth staff at Grace Baptist Church. When I think of the sacrifices you made simply because you love students, it still amazes me even today. From youth staff retreats in Radium to mission trips in Soledad, your gift of service to me still renders me speechless. We laughed together, prayed together, got in trouble together, and loved God and students together. I miss you guys.

Mark, a youth staff volunteer who taught me the value of knowing who you are created to be in Christ and how to serve out of that. You modeled to me through your tears the deep love you had for our students. To many of them, you were their dad.

Tyler, a youth staff volunteer who came into the office every day after working a full day simply because you knew I needed help. Thanks for modeling to me what it means to serve someone because you believe in that person.

Pastor Morel, a deep ministry friend who allowed our group to come to his church in Soledad, California, every summer and, as an eighty-plus year old, loved on the students I loved. You were such an inspiration and a deep ministry friend. I look forward to living near you in heaven.

Jeff, my first official intern, who was more gifted than I could ever dream of being. Your ability to let me lead you even though you knew how to figure it out without me was commendable. Thank you for letting me lead you.

Maris and Macauleigh, who are now a part of the Wilks youth group. The four of us have many memories to build upon. You both remind me how much a relationship with my family means, and I love spending time with you.

Jason and Tony, who were students in my youth ministry and then served on my team for many years at Grace Baptist Church. Because of you two, I first understood what a proud dad feels like when he looks at his kids. You are some of the most loyal and gifted guys around.

Sheryl, Wally, and John, who were staff members with me for many years and then let me lead them when I stepped into being their boss. I know it was difficult seeing the youth pastor become the lead pastor, but your support allowed me to do what God called me to do.

Students at Grace Baptist Church who allowed me to lead them and allowed me to speak into their lives for many years. It was a great journey, and I knew when I stepped into the lead pastor role that I was losing you. No one ever asked you to share your pastor, but you did it because you knew God was asking me to lead the church. Thanks for helping us lead the church.

Kevin, Anne, and Darren, who were members of the pastoral care committee charged with helping me. I loved getting together with you simply because I got to share my heart and hear yours. Nothing is greater in this world than knowing there are people who are more mature (in both wisdom and age) than you in your corner fighting for you. Thanks for trusting in me.

Dennis, a dear friend who always made sure I was doing well in life and ministry. Thank you for all those breakfast visits in Red Deer.

Congregation at Grace Baptist Church. I wasn't even old enough to be a board member, and still you let me be your lead pastor. I wasn't experienced, and yet you trusted I was being led by God as I led you.

Chris. For some reason, God brought us together in Chicago and started us on this journey. You have taught me so much in such a short time about business, theology, and loyalty. There are few bosses I respect deeply, and you are one of them. I value your friendship so much and wish God would orchestrate that we had more times together.

Youthfront. Mike, Topher, Dustin, Jim, Ray, Jamie, and Andy. All of you taught me so much about how to invest in students' lives in new ways. I loved the chance to have a relationship with you all that wasn't expected.

Life Development Team at Centre Street. I was beginning to miss working in the church and shaping a team, and God brought you all into my life. Thanks for letting me lead you in the process of developing a spiritual-formation strategy for infants to thirty year olds. You all were honest with me and let me shape you by trusting in me quickly.

Lake Windermere Alliance Church, my dear friends at my mountain retreat. Thanks for your encouragement and the opportunity to build relationships with you, a church full of people who love God and are working hard to figure out how to impact their community. I love this journey with you.

Camp Harmattan Summer Staff. This group of young adults brought an enormous amount of personal joy to me. This is a group of young people who love Jesus and love students. Thanks for letting me lead you!

Wayne, a current ministry partner and friend. God always brings people into our lives who balance us out, and your relational gifts are an inspiration to me.

Glimpses of all these relationships are contained in the pages that follow. I hope you see that this book wasn't written void of personal experience. This book is littered with mistakes I have made as well as a true desire to enter into a relationship with you.

You are called to be a youth worker, and this is the greatest call God can place on your life because you have the opportunity to shape a generation of students who will change the world.

Thanks for your contribution(s) to the students of this generation! May this book encourage you as you build relationships with them.

INTRODUCTION

Cultivate—to promote or improve the *growth of* by labor and attention; to foster within the context of a relationship

It has been an interesting journey as I have set out to write this book. The many different relationships a youth worker must manage are comprised of a large variety of people who each have unique and complex demands of a youth worker.

I started writing my thoughts on a piece of paper many years ago as I moved from being the youth pastor to the lead pastor in my church. There were things I wished I could go back and undo as I sat in the lead pastor's chair. There were relationships I had taken for granted and relationships I hadn't invested as much of myself in as I should have.

A couple years ago, I started writing what would become this book. In no way do I feel like an author or gifted communicator. But I do know that I would have loved to have had a book like this when I came out of college as a twenty-two-year-old youth pastor.

The last couple of years have seen me reengage in the local church context, redeploy a struggling camp, and have daughters who are now in middle school. These last few years have taught and reestablished for me the value of relationships within a Christian community, organization, and team. If we don't understand or value relationships the way we should, we may end up running from them. The goal of this book is to help us cultivate the community of youth workers so we can better understand the relationships God entrusts us with.

If you are a volunteer, the context of your relationships might be different, but there are concepts that will be valuable for you to understand in all the relationships you enjoy.

I wish we could just snap our fingers and make relationships work, but it truly takes time and wisdom, just like the time and wisdom it takes a farmer to cultivate the right crop.

The pages of this book will hopefully confront you, encourage you, and equip you as youth workers to:

- investigate the depth of your own personal relationships;
- understand the differences and values of each unique relationship you are a part of
- change the focus and depth of your relationships;
- move to a place of being proactive rather than reactive in your relationships.

I encourage you to come with a pencil or pen in your hand and an honest heart as together we evaluate our relationships.

On a personal note, I value you as a youth worker because of the relationships I formed with you as a kid in your youth ministry, as a young pastor serving your students at the beginning of my ministry journey with very little experience or wisdom, and now as the parent of a daughter who I am praying will continue to fall madly in love with Jesus through watching you.

Prayer*

Lord, make me an instrument of thy peace;
where there is hatred, let me sow love;
where there is injury, pardon;
where there is doubt, faith;
where there is despair, hope;
where there is darkness, light;
and where there is sadness, joy.

O Divine Master,
grant that I may not so much seek to be consoled
as to console;
to be understood, as to understand;
to be loved, as to love.

For it is in giving that we receive;
it is in pardoning that we are pardoned;
and it is in dying that we are born to eternal life.

*St. Francis of Assisi, 13th century

Cultivating Personal Relationships

Developing depth in our personal relationships is something we need to focus on before we can even begin to think of doing youth ministry. It can become so easy for us to be involved in the work of ministry yet forget the two most important relationships we have to care for.

The depth of our own personal walks with Jesus will be directly attached to the depth our youth ministries have with Jesus. There often seems to be a disconnect between what we ask our students, volunteers, and parents to do in their Christian walks as compared to what is evident in our own lives.

Ministry is a difficult balancing act for families. As we fall deeper in love with Jesus, we need to learn how to deepen the relationships we have with our families. Our families need to be our ministry priorities first as we model for students what healthy relationships within the context of a family *should* look like.

How do we lead out of a place of true balance between what ministry demands of us and what the relationships no one really sees require of us? How do we create an internal strategy that protects against the lack of care or focus in these relationships? What happens when we truly fall in love with God?

ONE

GOD

Intimacy—a close, familiar, and usually affectionate or loving
personal relationship with another person or group; simply
the quality of being comfortable, warm, or familiar

It should be easy, one might think, to cultivate a relationship with God
into a place of deep intimacy. After all, this is the foundation of what we
are called to, isn't it? Isn't it what we teach each week to the students in
our ministries?

Many of us have taken some level of education where we studied
theology. We know the answers in our heads but struggle to move those
answers to our hearts. I believe we want to have deep and intimate relationships with God, but in the work aspect of ministry, we worry about
everyone but ourselves.

At one time during my years in college, I looked back and figured
I had heard more than five thousand sermons. (Yes, some of you will
remember that, way back when, we actually had morning *and* evening
church!) We have heard thoughts from most of the pages of the Bible we
teach from, yet many youth workers seem to have shallow relationships
with Jesus.

There is a ritualistic approach now. We rush to read Scripture to
prepare for the next lesson (which should have been prepared a few days
ago). We pray out of duty, not a passion to intimately get to know the

23
*

Father's heart. We serve because we want the praise and affirmation of the people entrusted to our care.

≡ **How deep and intimate is your relationship with God?**

≡ **How can you become more intimate in your relationship with God?**

In the beautiful Rocky Mountains, on a youth staff retreat one time, a youth ministry volunteer once asked me, "How shallow and guarded is your relationship with God?" The question wrecked me because, as I began to evaluate the corporate youth pastor I had become, I saw how my own personal relationship with God had become exactly that—shallow and guarded.

I didn't want that type of relationship with God and certainly didn't want to model or teach that to my students, but that is what it had become. It had become something I had a good amount of knowledge in but which lacked personal passion. I could create a spiritual formation process for everyone under my care, but I didn't have time to get away with the Father.

Looking back, there were some pivotal times for me in this journey of understanding how to bring about depth and intimacy into my life as a leader of students; times and places in my life where God has asked me to rest and find my place in him. Let me share a couple with you.

I had just joined the staff team at Sonlife Ministries, and Chris Folmsbee had us meet a man named Scot McKnight. Scot had written *The Jesus Creed*, and this book was foundational in who and what Sonlife was becoming. Scot shared a definition in his book that is included in youth worker training materials that Chris has written. This definition continues to resonate with me as much as it did the first time I read it.

A disciple *is one who engages with Jesus as a person and because of that relationship begins to live out the virtues that Jesus talks about.*

I had to ask myself at that moment a simple question that I still ask myself daily: *How much trust do I have in my relationship with Jesus?*

The second time I was challenged in regards to the depth and intimacy of my relationship with God was when my daughter Maris entered the seventh grade. I could see she was watching me to see how deep my relationship was with God. I could tell she had questions that revolved around the general idea, *Is this for real?* and, *Does this work?* I have to be the one who can provide for her a real-life example of what falling in love with Jesus looks like.

≡ **What needs to change in your relationship with God?**

In Matthew 11:28-30, Jesus proclaims, "Come to me, all you who are weary and burdened, and I will give you rest. Take my yoke upon you and learn from me, for I am gentle and humble in heart, and you will find rest for your souls. For my yoke is easy and my burden is light."

Come to me and I will give you rest.

I love that Jesus is asking us to come rather than expecting us to work. It is so different from what we see all around us. There is no expectation but to come. As we explore the many different relationships we are a part of, the majority of them will expect that we give something of ourselves. It just isn't the same with God. He asks us to simply *come*.

We are allowed to come tired.

We are allowed to come broken.

We are allowed to come beaten up.

≡ **When was the last time you went to God for rest?**

≡ **How do you find true rest with God in the hustle and bustle of life?**

≡ **What does this look like in youth ministry for yourself, your volunteers, and your students?**

There is a passage of Scripture I remind myself of almost on a daily basis. Within this simple verse, we learn five deep truths about what God wants us to experience. These five truths help us develop the depth of our relationship with God.

As you read this next section, read it through once and then come back and pray this over yourself. Experience what God is saying to you and what he longs for you to experience.

Zephaniah 3:17: *The Lord your God is with you, he is mighty to save. He will take great delight in you, he will quiet you with his love, he will rejoice over you with singing.*

The Lord your God is with you. It is no surprise that, when Jesus was on earth, he continually went to his Father to get his strength. It was a reminder to Jesus that the Father was with him, that he hadn't abandoned him. God the Father goes with us as we face those frustrated-parent meetings or the daily grind of ministry.

He is mighty to save. God proclaims a message to us that he *wants* to save us—not simply from our sin but from the pain of this world. As ministry comes fast, furiously, and frustratingly at us, we need to call out to our Father, who longs to save us.

He will take great delight in you. God is proud of you before you do anything. You can't earn more or less of God's love. In Mark 1, at Christ's baptism, we see God the Father appearing in the form of a dove and simply uttering, "You are my son, whom I love; with you I am well pleased." The interesting thing is that Jesus hasn't done anything yet. He has just been a good son of a carpenter. God is saying the same things to us: *I am proud of you, and you can't earn more or less of my love.*

He will quiet you with his love. Jesus needs those quiet moments with God to simply hear his Father's voice. It is in those quiet moments that we hear God's voice as well as experience God's endless love. It is critical for us, as we get busy in ministry, to have those quiet moments when we hear God's still, small voice.

He will rejoice over you with singing. God has a song for you that he wants to sing over you. Just as my wife, when our daughters were young, sang a special song to quiet them, God has a song for you. It is a song full of love and peace to rejoice over you, his creation.

≡ What do you need from God today?

Take a moment, reread the previous section, and ask him for what you need. Where is your refuge?

God longs for us to understand this simple truth found in Psalm 34:8: "Taste and see that the Lord is good; blessed is the man who takes refuge in him."

———

A high school student came and made a deeply profound comment to me after a weekly Bible study we were having. She simply looked at me and said, "I would love to do that, Pastor Matt, but I need you to show me how."

So often in our relationships with God, we put things on autopilot and just move along through the routines of life. But the people under our care desperately need to see us madly in love with the Father.

Yes, our relationships with God are private, but all we know those people who are madly in love with the Father. In my life, my parents are a perfect example of this. Their deep love for God can be seen in what they say, the advice they give, and how they spend their time. Our relationships with God must be modeled to our students in such a way that they see God at work in our lives.

Ancient Celtic Prayer*

God to enfold me,
God to surround me.
God in my speaking,
God in my thinking.

God in my sleeping,
God in my waking,
God in my watching,
God in my hoping.

God in my life,
God in my lips,
God in my soul,
God in my heart.

God in my sufficing,
God in my slumber,
God in mine ever-living soul,
God in mine eternity.

---

*Collected by Alexander Carmichael (1832-1912); published in *Carmina Gadelica* (Edinburgh: Floris Books, 1992)

FAMILY

I have been married for seventeen years, and I am still growing in my love for my wife, Michelle. She is an incredible woman of God who inspires me deeply in my walk with God as well as my relationships with other people.

Michelle works for an organization in Calgary. The program she is involved with focuses on caring for high-risk new moms who don't have healthy support networks around them. This job inspires her because she is paid to give these new moms a few hours off to sleep, go for a run, or do whatever they need to do in order to rest and recharge. She loves it and is good at it.

I have two daughters—Maris, who is a few months away from being a teenager (yes, I have prayed God would return before that happened), and Macauleigh, who has just joined us in the double digits at ten!

I have become a jack of all trades in regards to my family. If necessary, I can straighten Maris's naturally curly hair or curl Macauleigh's straight hair. There are times in my house when emotions are at an all-time high, but I love being with my girls.

As youth workers, one of the most important areas of our lives we need to cultivate is our families. There are few things I want to be remembered by other than that I had a deep love for God, I served him with a reckless abandon, and I loved my family deeply.

≣ How cared for by you does your family feel right now?
(Hint: Ask your family!)

≣ What special events do you plan for your family to create lifetime
memories with them?

We all have a visual grid in our heads of the priorities in our lives.
We know the right answers of God first, families second, and ministry third, but so often, ministry takes over. It isn't intentional, but we
believe (out of an unhealthy fear) that if we don't succeed in ministry,
then we have failed everyone.

Our families become whom we expect to hold it all together so we
can do ministry. We unintentionally place a noose around our families'
necks as we go care for the people we are paid to care for.

There are some definite mistakes I made in my first twelve years of
ministry that I work hard every day now not to repeat.

Expectation Mindset

In a ministry environment, we feel that everyone's expectations need
to be met. Whether it is a large ministry setting or a small one, it is
impossible for you to be everything to everyone. In reality, most people
have little or no expectations of you. Usually these expectations are created in our own minds as we pursue what we believe is the definition of
what a pastor should do. I know I found myself feeling like I was on the
hamster wheel, running incredibly hard and going nowhere fast.

≣ What expectations do you believe people have put on you? Talk to
someone in leadership about these to see if they are true.

Savior Mindset

An elderly member of my church in Calgary once grabbed me by the
arm and simply said these profound words to me: "Jesus already came to
save the world, Matt. He doesn't need you to save it again. He just needs
you to contribute to it." There is an interesting transition that happens

when we have ministry success. We believe (even though we might not say it) that the success is tied directly to us and that we have to keep performing, or it will disappear.

≡ Where has the Savior mindset crept into your ministry?

Not-Enough-Hours Mindset

A board member once told me rather directly, when I was complaining about the hours I was working, that no one expected, wanted, or demanded the kind of hours I was working. Driving home that day, I remember asking myself a few things about the board member's statement. But the point wasn't in diagnosing the solution. It was simply to be able to get hold of my priorities, and my number-one priority needed to be my home. Ministry is one of those jobs where we can fall into the trap of giving our best to everyone else and bringing our leftovers home.

≡ Are you always tired when you come home? What is the average number of hours you have worked per week over the last few months?

Chaos Mindset

Some of us love to be organized while others love the thrill of the mess (or what we like to call the adventure). In ministry, chaos can show its ugly head in many different forms. It can show up in the way we schedule things in our day planners, the way we leave projects to the last minute, or even in the way we conduct the hours we are physically in the office. One of the biggest distractions for us in life can be us simply giving ourselves to good things while keeping ourselves away from the great things.

≡ How have you contributed to the chaos in your life? Is your life ordered or a mess?

24-Hour-Accessibility Mindset

We are incredibly connected in the world today, what with our Blackberries, iPhones, Skype, and the wealth of other gadgets and interfaces that keep us, essentially, connected at the hip. But the issue with all of these tools is that seldom do we shut them down. For many years, my laptop sat on my lap in the family room as we hung out together. It was then replaced by my Blackberry, which fits nicely with my wife and me on the couch. My excuse has simply been that I didn't want to leave a "pile" of emails I would have to answer in the morning. But something interesting has happened. My wife's Blackberry has joined us on the couch, and the girls' iPod Touches are now beside them. Unfortunately, this could lead to us growing disconnected from one another. My efforts to stay connected to my ministry have modeled a disconnected relationship to my family.

≡ **What other mindsets have crept into who you are that steals time away from your family? What mindsets do you currently struggle with?**

Part of the Solution

I am in the same boat as many, if not all, of you when it comes to our schedules and where our families fit in. To be honest, I am the guy who suddenly began leading men's ministry because I saw a lack of leadership. I was the guy who gave everything to everyone then brought the leftovers home.

My family knew I loved them, but I have found myself using the excuse that I am growing the ministry the way God wants me to, and it takes time. I have even bought into the excuse that one day—once I have it all organized and functioning—*then* I would be able to spend more time at home. This was just the beginning of what became an unhealthy pattern.

I wasn't able to get a handle on my schedule until I learned a way to organize my week into a really simple, manageable technique that allowed me to guard my time with my family.

Grab a piece of paper and divide each day of your week into three large blocks with Morning, Afternoon, and Evening. Each day needs its own set of three blocks, which will give you twenty-one blocks for the entire week.

Now, begin to block out the times you are *required* to be somewhere (e.g., your job, small group, Sunday morning church). Your goal is to find at least five spots when you have no requirements or expectations to be somewhere. Once you get a handle on a schedule with at least five spots available, you need to make it your goal to get to seven spots where you can rest and enjoy time with God and your family.

	Morning	Afternoon	Evening
Sunday			
Monday			
Tuesday			
Wednesday			
Thursday			
Friday			
Saturday			

≡ **How does your priority list elevate your family to the important place they need to be?**

≡ **What are the ministry things that take you away from your family that you need to work to eliminate from your schedule?**

≡ **What do you need to do so your family knows you value them just as much as your ministry?**

As I approach the age of forty, I have learned that my two girls don't really care what job title their dad has or where their dad has been asked to speak or how big their dad's ministry is. What they do care about is simply, *Is my dad picking me up from school?* or, *Is my dad coaching my sports team?* I have learned that my wife merely wants me to be a partner in the home—helping to cook meals, vacuuming and picking up where I can, and watching some TV shows that just let our minds wander away from the events of the day.

I want to be known as a man of God who loves Maris, Macauleigh, and Michelle the way Jesus calls me to love. I want them to remember times when we, as a family, laughed, cried, and enjoyed being together. I want them to know that nothing is as important as they are.

Prayer*

O God, perfect us in love,
That we may conquer all selfishness and hatred of others;
Fill our hearts with thy joy,
And shed abroad in them thy peace which passeth understanding;
That so those murmurings and disputings
To which we are too prone may be overcome.
Make us long-suffering and gentle,
And thus subdue our hastiness and angry tempers,
And grant that we may bring forth the blessed fruits of the Spirit,
To thy praise and glory, through Jesus Christ our Lord.
Amen.

34
✳

---

*Reverend Henry Alford (1810-1871)

2

Cultivating Relationships within the Church

Coming out of a proper understanding of the depth we need in our relationships both with God and our families, we can then move to understand how to deepen our relationships with the different groups of people in our churches.

Each of us has a supervisor who leads us as we do ministry within a set of policies that have been dictated by our job descriptions or by others in the church. Our supervisor might be the senior or lead pastor or someone else on staff. It is imperative that we understand and learn what a healthy and productive relationship looks like with our supervisor.

It can be easy to be so focused on our own ministries that we fail to develop relationships outside the routine of youth ministry. If we have the privilege of working on a multiple-staff-member team, we need to develop our skills as members of the team rather than constructing a ministry silo.

Our primary job is to help students grow in their relationships with Jesus. For most of us, this is one of the main reasons we felt God called us to work with students. It is important for us to understand the different relationships students desire from us, their youth workers. The differences we have in relationships give us the opportunity to develop students into healthy contributors to the mission of God here on earth.

The majority of a student's time is spent in relationships outside the walls of the church. One of the greatest resources for accomplishing what we desire for the students in our youth ministry is to learn how to partner with their parents in a way that is productive and not combative. Parents can be some of your greatest resources for your youth ministry.

Youth ministry demands a large amount of individuals who are committed to the spiritual transformation of the students under their care. God will only give us the number of students we will be good stewards of. It is vitally important that we as youth pastors invest an enormous amount of time developing the team that will help minister to the students under our care. These volunteers are the representatives of the love of Jesus to these students.

Some youth ministries will be privileged to have interns or summer students working with them. One of the most important aspects for us in regards to these emerging leaders is that we model for them what it means to be called by God to do the work of God. So often, we focus on the skills of ministry rather than developing the heart for ministry. Our effectiveness in developing the next generation of church leaders is paramount to the lessons taught in our internship programs.

All of these relationships involve us as youth workers working hard to understand all their unique complexities. Working through developing relationships in the church can be understood as playing the game of golf. Our golf bag contains many different clubs that come in different shapes and different degrees of angles, yet the swing is still the same. For each one of these relationships, the swing is the same. Our goal is to learn how to effectively cultivate and grow each of these relationships.

THREE

SUPERVISOR

In my career inside and outside the church, I have been both an employee and a supervisor. I have been in settings where I worked my way up the ladder and became the supervisor of staff members who weren't pleased with my advancement.

I have had great bosses and bosses who were not so great. There have been supervisors who completely stayed out of my way and others who had a very short rope on my leadership.

You will encounter a variety of leadership styles as you lead your youth ministry. For some of you, your supervisor will be your senior pastor or another staff member while, for others of you, it might be your church board or another committee.

Unfortunately, many times there is a distinct disconnect between ourselves and our supervisors, which causes our effectiveness and longevity to be cut shorter than it needs to be.

My Story

The summer of 1994 was an exciting one for me. It all started on May 14, as I married my wife, Michelle, a week after we graduated from Crown College. I had my degree in youth ministry in hand and a desire to simply shoot hoops with kids in the gym of the church and a dream of hopefully impacting them positively for Jesus when all was said and done.

A week later, Michelle and I were on a yellow school bus, off to our first youth retreat, and the youth ministry journey began. A month later, my supervising youth pastor patted me on the back and said he would be gone for two months and that this was the best internship possible for me because I would be learning firsthand without him around.

That summer involved me making a wealth of mistakes, trying to figure out how to balance ministry and a new wife, with a supervisor who was nowhere to be found.

The fall of 1994 saw a senior pastor contact me from a Baptist church in Calgary that was interested in hiring me to be the youth pastor. The interview process involved a glass of chocolate milk at a coffee shop and a few simple questions. For three and a half years, I had the privilege to learn from a senior pastor who was nearing the end of his ministry career.

Four years into my time at this church, a new senior pastor was hired, and he was completely different from my first supervisor. This senior pastor had read up on all the corporate strategies and systems, and you either liked him or you didn't. He took us into a building project, and his popularity began to wane shortly after.

Our church was struggling with unity, and in a fairly quick time period, I moved from being the youth pastor to leading the church as the interim senior pastor. My world was changed, and I went from being supervised to being the one who supervised the entire operation.

The only thing I knew to do was work to eliminate the hidden things that seem to be prevalent in the church in North America: gossip, slander, distrust, and fighting among people who are called to love one another and God.

I stayed there for four more years as the lead pastor and eventually was a part of finding my replacement. Those years were pivotal in my development and caused me to wrestle through many of the thoughts included in this book. They were truly some of the greatest moments of my life.

A Few Choice Words about Supervisors

There are a few things you need to remind yourself on a regular basis:

- You need a supervisor.
- A supervisor is there to help you succeed.
- A healthy respect for your supervisor is what God calls leaders to have.

A couple of men named Fred and Doug from my church took me, a twenty-three-year-old youth pastor, out for breakfast one morning. I was sharing how my frustration was mounting with the senior pastor, who didn't seem to listen to me and who was so out of touch with what I saw as real ministry.

These men looked at me and quickly said in the nicest way they could, "Matt, you need to respect our senior pastor because God called him to the church as our leader. You need to respect him in your words and how you refer to him. Your greatest mark of success isn't how big you build your youth ministry but simply how much you respect those who lead you. You are called to model that to us and to your students."

Those simple yet profound words shaped my view of future supervisors and how I conducted the way I would work at the church. I think one of the misconceptions we have in ministry is that we are either friends or enemies with our supervisors. I am confident that we are neither.

I guarantee you will have a spectacular supervisor as well as a poor supervisor in the course of your ministry career. I have had many supervisors, and each of them in some way has contributed to who I am. Some have allowed me to soar while others have taught me lessons on respect and call and God's plan.

There are many factors that go into understanding how to function, cooperate, and find success with the people who supervise us. The key is to realize that they are called by God for such a time as this.

One of the most important things for us to consider is to learn to identify what kind of supervisor you have and how to function underneath that type of leadership.

41
*

There are all kinds of great leadership books out there that will help you wrestle through how to find success in the role you have been given with the supervisor who has been called to lead you.

Let me give you a brief synopsis of three different kinds of supervisors I have had in the ministry settings I have been a part of.

Corporate, Charismatic Supervisor

Usually this person is viewed as the glue that holds the organization together, and success (or failure) has come because of this individual. Stories are told of how great this individual is, and everyone is in awe of his or her leadership abilities.

This type of supervisor loves leading. Decisions are made by consulting very few people. Final decisions are delegated to others to implement.

Success:	The easiest way to succeed with a corporate type of leader is to make sure you fully understand the mission and vision he or she believes God has called the ministry to. Reports with clear and quantitative results please this type of leader.
Question:	How do I and my ministry area help accomplish the mission or vision of the church?
Praise:	You will know you have succeeded in the eyes of this individual when you hear him or her praise you in front of other prominent figures and when he or she uses the statistics from your reports.
Your Best Move:	Invest time in your reports to make them as detailed as you can.

Decisions are made quickly and usually involve some frustration on the part of the people underneath.

They love systems and flowcharts that show where everyone fits into the organization. This kind of leader is usually knowledgeable on the latest leadership book and movement that is happening both in the church and the corporate world. Leadership accountability is done through reports that document quantitative measurements.

Shepherding, People-Oriented Supervisor

Usually this person is viewed as the chief shepherd, friend to all. This supervisor knows everyone's name and what is going on in each person's life. A shepherd supervisor looks out at the congregation each Sunday and can see exactly who is missing.

This type of supervisor is passionate about the care of the people. Decisions are made with the individual's needs in mind first. Decisions can be slow at times.

They love people and use people as the evaluation grid for gauging your effectiveness as a leader. Most of their time is spent with people, caring for and helping them. Strategic plans come second to the care of

Success:	The easiest way to succeed with a people-oriented leader is to care deeply for the people they have entrusted to your care. Every action and decision you make has to be made with people in mind.
Question:	How am I providing care to the people my supervisor has entrusted to me?
Praise:	You will know you have succeeded in the eyes of these individuals when you hear them tell your stories of impact.
Your Best Move:	Invest time in telling them verbal stories of impact that you are observing in your ministry.

their people. Leadership accountability is measured by stories from individuals about the care you have provided for them and their families.

Team, Democratic Supervisor

Usually this person operates by using a team to make every decision. This person functions as the supervisor but leads in an empowerment style.

This type of supervisor loves meetings and loves collaborating on projects. Much time is spent in meetings and building relationships with the team. Decisions will be made but will take longer than necessary because of the value placed on everybody being heard.

Reporting will be done through meetings and making sure everyone has a chance to share as a team. Retreats, prayer days, conferences, and multi-day experiences are very much a part of this leadership style.

Success:	Your presence and input are critical for this leader to feel you are contributing to the team. A calendar that is open for collaborative exercises as a team is important to this leader.
Question:	How am I contributing to the success of the team?
Praise:	You will know you have succeeded in the eyes of this individual when proof can be given that decisions have been made as a collective team, not as individuals.
Your Best Move:	Attend the meetings called. Be fully engaged in the discussions. Find ways to contribute outside your specific piece of the ministry.

44
*

≡ What kind of supervisor do you currently have?

≡ How have you struggled? How have you found success?

☰ **What do you need to change to find success with your supervisor?**

☰ **What do you need from your supervisor? Commit to telling him or her.**

One of the hardest things in ministry is learning the dance in how to be led. We all have great ideas that we believe will change the world and also change the church to be what it needs to be in this world.

The way we learn to interact with our supervisor is one of the ways we honor the people whom God has put in authority over us. Our students need to see that we respect authority and the people God has placed in leadership over us.

Prayer*

Servants, do what you're told by your earthly masters. And don't just do the minimum that will get you by. Do your best. Work from the heart for your real Master, for God, confident that you'll get paid in full when you come into your inheritance. Keep in mind always that the ultimate Master you're serving is Christ. The sullen servant who does shoddy work will be held responsible. Being a follower of Jesus doesn't cover up bad work.

45
✳

---

*Colossians 3:22-25 (MSG)

FOUR

BOARD OF ELDERS

Who are these guys? Do they meet behind closed doors and make decisions without anyone knowing what they have decided? Do they even know who I am?

Depending on the size of your church or the structure of your church's leadership model, you will be faced with many different perceptions or even misconceptions with your board.

The board or leadership committee can be something that can cause a lot of frustrations with a youth pastor or youth ministry. They can be viewed as dictators or simply people who are making decisions void of relationships. The reality is that many elder or leadership teams actually protect you as a leader when misunderstandings or struggles come into your ministry life.

It is vitally important for a youth pastor or youth leader to work to develop relationships with the board or leadership committee. Many times, fear enters into our minds, which leads to a protective attitude that causes us to be distant from the leadership team.

In many churches, the board makes decisions that affect the youth ministry directly. Unfortunately these decisions are sometimes made void of a relational composition that helps the board understand how to support the youth ministry in being all that God has called it to be.

As a leader in the church, it is important that you take the time to understand the model of leadership your church uses. It is not the same in every church or denomination, and by simply investing time in understanding the model of leadership that your church uses, you can eliminate the confusion and anguish of your board's influence on your youth ministry.

Ask yourself these simple questions and take time to read up on your church's leadership structure.

≣ **What model of leadership does your church use? Is it led by a board, or is the senior pastor the large decision maker?**

≣ **Does the congregation play a large role in making decisions?**

≣ **Can the senior pastor make a decision above the board? What position does the senior pastor have on the board?**

≣ **Is the board a policy governance board or a supervisory board?**

(Policy governance was created by John Carver, where the board is responsible for the ends and the staff is responsible for the means, while a supervisory model is one where accountability is in the means.)

There are some simple steps to effectively function as a youth ministry with the leadership board in your church. These steps will cause the lines of communication and understanding with your board to be effective and fruitful for many years to come.

Within the structure of the board or leadership team, there are different portfolios or positions that each member will hold. These positions can range from secretary to finance to building or even into specific ministry positions. The main difference from an organizational structure is that these relationships could change every year or every few years. It is important for a youth ministry to invest time in understanding the different roles or portfolios each person who makes up the leadership team or board holds.

48
*

So often, the leadership team within the church can provide the help needed to navigate many of the issues that arise within the context of youth ministry. By understanding the board portfolios, a youth ministry leader will know with whom to cast vision and from whom to ask specific advice.

Learn how to communicate with them. Focus on the relational connectedness that each of them brings to the table rather than the accountability that comes only from the positions they hold.

≣ **What are the different roles that people hold on your church's leadership team?**

≣ **Who are these people away from the church? What are they good at? What do they enjoy doing?**

The board or leadership team functions as the primary source of accountability for the congregation and the staff. The board is challenged to hold the staff accountable, usually through the leadership of the senior pastor, but that does not remove the accountability from the board for the youth pastor.

So often as youth pastors, we seek to have no relationship or accountability with the board since we believe it will benefit us not to have "two bosses." I want to encourage you to push back against that mindset a little bit.

There are some easy ways for you to forge accountability with the board or leadership team that will benefit you and your ministry in the long run.

Fiscal Accountability

Usually this is the area that causes the youth ministry or youth pastor a lot of grief and frustration. We never feel like we have enough money, and usually we have lost a receipt or two.

I have had many different leaders during my time as a youth pastor. Some were very hands off in regard to finances while others wanted every pencil to be accounted for. One of the keys in the area of finances is to understand the parameters in which you are called to function.

The bottom line is simply this: If the board trusts you with how you spend the church's money, they will certainly trust you with more things than just the money.

Do you remember the parable of the talents? Whom are you most like? The individual who had ten coins and earned ten more or the one who had one coin and buried it out of fear of his boss?

≡ **What are some ways that you can become even more transparent in regard to the area of finances?**

≡ **How do you ask for finances, and how well do you share the resources your youth ministry has?**

Facility Accountability

How many of us in youth ministry have put a hole in the wall or broken a glass window? I had the great pleasure of being able to oversee a tree knocked down in the parking lot, many holes being put in many different walls, and almost filling the church's sanctuary with the two truckloads of sand I carted in for the annual beach night in our gym.

Youth ministries have a notorious history of being in opposition to the people who care for the facilities of the church. Whether it is right or wrong, the perception is that the youth ministry does not take care of the facilities that God has entrusted to the church. Unfortunately, youth ministries do not normally take the initiative in being proactive rather than reactive with facility accountability.

A youth ministry that has healthy relationships in regards to facility accountability is one that asks before using the facility for another round of turkey bowling. The best move a youth ministry can make is to plan ahead and communicate extensively with the people who are in leadership for care of the facility.

≡ What is your current relationship with the facility leadership team at your church? What can you do to improve it and build upon a healthy relationship?

≡ How are you at being a good steward with the facility that God has given to you?

Policy Accountability

I don't think anyone is a huge fan of rules and regulations, but at the heart of policies is the desire to provide a structure that protects the individual or ministry group. As youth workers, we need to work hard to protect ourselves within the boundaries that are set up for us.

Youth workers have a tendency to operate with rebellion toward policy. We don't want to be contained or forced into a corner, and we feel that policies put the shackles on us.

Instead of feeling restricted by policies, we need to feel empowered by them. By learning to be accountable within the framework of the policies that are designed to protect us, we show a certain respect to the leadership of the church.

≡ What policies in your church do you personally struggle with? Do you struggle with these because of an issue in your own life?

≡ How can you rebuild trust with your leadership team in regard to the policies that are in your church?

Finally, as youth workers, the greatest way for us to develop a deep working relationship with the leadership team or board in our church is to ask for a clear job description and expectations. So often, in our roles at the church, there is confusion about what we are perceived to be doing and what we need to be doing.

Many times in churches or organizations, we get hired for specific roles that were present at the time we were hired and don't exist anymore or have changed dramatically since then. It is important to get clarity about what we are currently hired to do, since it can change. This should be a conversation that regularly occurs between ourselves and the leadership of the church. Do not fear this conversation because it provides the outlet for us to help shape our current roles and responsibilities as well as serve the church in the most effective manner.

God can call us through this process to another position within the church, in our current ministry, or another position outside the walls of the church. One of the worst leadership strategies is to stay in a position longer than God has called us to. It affects relationships within and outside the church family.

Do not be afraid to bridge the conversation with your leadership team regarding your role and responsibilities in the church. As Stephen Covey has said, "Seek first to understand then to be understood." This is a great practice for youth pastors within the church to have success long term in their ministries.

To have a healthy relationship with the board or leadership team in the church, it is critical that we invest time in relationships with these teams. These relationships take time to develop and are critical to the success of the youth worker. Each month, take out board members or leadership team members for coffee or sit in their homes so you can learn more about who they are and they can learn more about who you are.

Together, model to the church what a healthy respect for leadership is and how leadership can work hand in hand to accomplish what God has in store for the church.

Prayer*

(1) Pray for your leaders privately. In all your quiet times with God, pray for your leaders that God would protect them and guide them as they serve you and the church.

> *God, I pray that you would give the leadership of the church a spiritual wisdom that you tell us to ask for if we lack.* (James 1)

(2) Pray *with* your leaders. Take time out of your busy schedules. As you pray with your leaders, pray specifically for the needs you believe they have outside their leadership responsibilities at church. Make sure to involve people who volunteer and support you in youth ministry.

> *God, I pray that you would allow the leaders to be transparent with one another and that you would allow them not to function outside of community but feel the love and appreciation of the community of believers.*

(3) Pray publicly for your leaders. Spread the word about the importance of praying for your leaders and model this as you pray for your leaders in a church service, meeting, or small-group gathering.

> *God, I pray for our leaders, that you would cause them to stay united in the decisions they make. Allow them to serve out of pure hearts that are focused on who you are and what you want for the church.*

53
*

---

*Adapted from: *Youth Leader's Academy*, "Serving your Leaders: Pray"

STAFF MEMBERS

It is our natural tendency as humans. We all want to be noticed for our hard work, and we all want to climb whatever perceived ladders there may be within the organizations we work for.

It started when James and John asked Jesus for the best seats in the kingdom in Mark 10:35-45:

> Then James and John, the sons of Zebedee, came to him. "Teacher," they said, "we want you to do for us whatever we ask." "What do you want me to do for you?" he asked. They replied, "Let one of us sit at your right and the other at your left in your glory." "You don't know what you are asking," Jesus said. "Can you drink the cup I drink or be baptized with the baptism I am baptized with?" "We can," they answered. Jesus said to them, "You will drink the cup I drink and be baptized with the baptism I am baptized with, but to sit at my right or left is not for me to grant. These places belong to those for whom they have been prepared." When the ten heard about this, they became indignant with James and John. Jesus called them together and said, "You know that those who are regarded as rulers of the Gentiles lord it over them, and their high officials exercise authority over them. Not so with you. Instead, whoever wants to become great among you must be your servant, and whoever wants to be first must be slave of all. For even the Son of Man did not come to be served, but to serve, and to give his life as a ransom for many."

So often in my life, I fall into the same boat as James and John. Questions abound in my head that simply end up leading me to a place I shouldn't go.

Questions like:

- Why is that staff member getting paid more than me?
- Does anyone notice all the "overtime" hours youth ministry requires of me?
- Why does that staff member get to communicate from the front?
- Why am I the only staff member who gets into trouble?
- Is anyone else on this team required to do the things I am asked to do?

≡ **What questions do you find yourself asking at times in regards to other staff members?**

Some of my greatest times in ministry have been when I have worked on a team. I have been a part of healthy teams, and there are certainly teams that have had their issues. I firmly believe God desires us to learn how to function as individuals working on a team. There have been some times when I have been a great teammate and some times when I have certainly been a very poor teammate.

Here are some common areas where we tend to fail as members of a larger staff team:

Silo Mentality

This is the most common way individuals begin to become ineffective as a team. Our minds tell us we were hired for a specific role, and we quickly realize that much of our worth can come from how people perceive success in our ministry area.

There is no harm in working incredibly hard in the ministry area we have been given responsibility for. The issue begins when we don't understand our place in the bigger picture of the church.

56
*

Symptoms of the silo mentality:

– Staff meetings become times when we are physically present but contribute nothing of value to the meetings.

– We find ourselves starting to recruit volunteers from other ministry areas and use the excuse that these individuals were called to serve in a different ministry.

Prescriptions for the silo mentality:

– Contribute fully in any staff meeting by sharing your passion, your thought processes, and your resources with the team.

– Discover the needs of other ministries and see if there are areas where you can help others out.

Poor-Me Mentality

When we function on a team, it is easy for us to have the *poor-me* mentality, which often finds it roots in times of failure or struggle but can also be found in times when the ministry is flourishing.

Hear this: *There will never be a time when everything will be completely fair on a team.* There are personality differences, ministry comfort levels, passions, and a wealth of other factors that contribute to the level of unfairness. The ability we develop to navigate those understandings can provide health on a staff team.

Symptoms of the poor-me *mentality:*

– Conversations with people inside and outside the ministry involve us talking down or comparing ourselves to other ministries. We use words and phrases such as, "If only I had…" or, "Our church cares about _____, not about students."

– We play the comparison game at staff meetings and try to one-up the stories of the next person so people view us as superior or more effective.

Prescriptions for the **poor-me** *mentality:*

— Institute the *Never tear down; always build up* mantra for any conversations that happen about other staff members or staff ministry areas.

— Learn to celebrate the ministry successes of other staff members so you have a relationship to share during times of pain in ministry.

Golden Calf Mentality

I remember sitting in a meeting with some ministry friends and thinking something along the lines of *Don't people understand that youth ministry is the place where real ministry takes place?* Let me explain.

In my perspective at that time, I felt that children's ministry got all the good stuff. They got the new computers, the new rooms in buildings, the cute baby dedications, and on and on. Youth ministry, on the other hand, seemed to get all the scraps or remnants—the hand-me-down couches, the lectures about holes in the walls, and the discussions about students who have piercings and tattoos.

I knew that if I could only have all those things the children's ministry was able to have, then I would be able to have ministry success. I began to chase the illusion of needing something I didn't have in order to have ministry success. I was trading in the Holy Spirit's work of transforming lives for needing *stuff* to ensure my success.

Symptoms of the golden calf mentality:

— Focus is on what we don't have, the needs we have, and what everyone else has.

— Focus that youth ministry is the only ministry really doing anything in the church.

Prescriptions for the golden calf mentality:

— Realization that the Holy Spirit is the supreme resource for the effectiveness of any ministry area.

– Realization that the effectiveness of a student ministry begins in children's ministry. Children's ministry is the foundation for youth ministry.

≡ **What mentality do you struggle with on a regular basis?**

≡ **What do you need to do to effectively combat this mentality?**

The way you function on a team inspires students and volunteers to be part of something bigger. The health of a team can contribute to calling people to a life of ministry, whether it is a full-time, paid position or a lifetime volunteer.

There are some simple principles that can help in your effectiveness with other staff members.

Whole-Self Contribution

There have been many times when I felt that some of my best ideas and concepts were given to someone else to run with. The reality is that you are called to be part of a team, and a team needs to win rather than an individual. Make sure—when you have team meetings, retreats, and getaways—that you contribute your whole self rather than just saving thoughts or ideas so you can get full credit at a later time.

Open Hands

It is critical that, as we function on a team, we model what it means to hold onto our resources lightly. If God is blessing another ministry area, we need to make sure we are not hoarding our resources because we don't want to share. Be known as a teammate who shares with open hands.

Relationally Connected

There are staff members whom you will want to spend time with and, of course, other staff members whom you would rather not spend any time with. One of the great aspects of working in a church together is that everyone has the opportunity to contribute to God's work

59
*

unfolding in your specific environment or location. We are all connected through story, and one of the most powerful ways to connect with other staff members is to hear their unique stories. Through the bond of story sharing, God can unite even the hardest personalities into a smoothly functioning team.

The greatest image in the Bible of how a team functioned well is the story of Moses's hands being held up by Aaron and Hur. It is found in Exodus 17, and God simply uses the image of Aaron and Hur holding Moses's hand up to guarantee success for Joshua and the Israeli army.

Are you known as the staff member who is committed to holding up someone else's arms?

≣ **What is your contribution to the staff team you are currently a part of?**

≣ **What do you need to receive from the team you are a part of?**

≣ **Whose arms on your staff team do you need to commit to holding up?**

One of the greatest joys in ministry comes when you find your place and see clearly your contribution to a team. I miss the times of brainstorming and collaboration that were so much a part of my formative years as a youth pastor.

Prayer*

Lord, we ask you to preside over our meetings and our labours, and to bless all our endeavours.

Help us to build a community united in harmony of love and service.

We thank you, Lord, for everything which widens our knowledge and equips us more fully for the task of life and living.

Teach us to know our own strengths, that we may use to the full the gifts and talents which you have given us.

Help us to share a loving concern for each other at all times.

Above all, Lord, help us to really know you, for this is the beginning and the end of all wisdom; this is eternal life.

*Anonymous

SIX

STUDENTS

Working with students is by far one of the greatest calls that can be placed on us. The opportunity to shape what the next generation of Christ followers will look like is both an honor and an enormous challenge.

Students need healthy adults in their lives who can take them places they haven't yet been. Students want to be noticed for their contributions to the world they live in, but they need you to help them.

People outside of youth ministry ask us when we will grow up and be a real pastor. We constantly are working to repair the tree that got knocked down in the parking lot or the hole that now has appeared in the wall by the sanctuary. The music we listen to and the way we do ministry is so foreign to everyone outside youth ministry that we simply give up trying to explain what we do. Yet, in spite of this, we love students because we see something in students that others fail to see: potential. Potential is the motivation for youth workers when students make the wrong choices or have more ups and downs than a hot air balloon.

One year at Sonlife Ministries, we partnered with an organization called Authentic Leadership. This organization is led by an incredible leader named Dan Webster. Dan taught me so many things about leadership and the ability each of us has to negatively or positively affect people.

Dan made this comment when we were sitting at Red Robin in Denver, Colorado. "It is incredibly important for us as youth workers to put the resources we have at our disposal into the students we have. Instead of us taking all the glory and doing the things we think we need to do, we need to get on the team of these students and give them the resources we have."

I am sure you're thinking of the adults in your life who made a profound impact on who you are. I have been blessed in my life with a variety of different individuals who have helped me become who I am today.

There are all kinds of programmed events and activities that can impact students. These are the events a youth ministry uses to get a boost or to begin to effect change in students' lives. But events and activities have short-term benefits and are not focused on long-term change.

The difference when ministry leaders focus on imparting their lives into students is found when they work toward creating a sustainable and manageable set of values for which students can order their lives.

To impart your life to a student takes a lot more time, effort, and focus than creating an event that affects a larger group of people. If we want to correct the trend of students leaving the church in their young adult years, we have to move to a place of imparting our lives to these students rather than impacting them with our programming.

≡ **What is the difference in your programming between impacting a group of students and imparting your life to them?**

≡ **Is there harm if a youth ministry just focuses on impacting a group of students?**

≡ **What does current youth ministry need to focus its efforts on?**

———

Throughout the next few pages of this chapter, I encourage you to grab a pen and write down names of students who come to mind as you read these words. These are students you care deeply for, and this will serve as a reminder to you of why you do youth ministry the way you do.

There are a variety of different relationships we enjoy with students. Some of these relationships will be dependent on the stage of life we are in, and some of them will be based on the type of relationship the student needs at his or her phase of life.

In our training at Barefoot Ministries, we ask a simple question about the different roles we perform in youth ministry. The answers we hear range from ATM to taxi driver to dating counselor to spiritual guide.

The realization is that you will not be able to personally be all of these roles to every student who comes into your youth ministry. This needs to motivate us to recruit a team of passionate people who love God and love students, but it also needs to challenge us to serve out of the uniqueness of who God has called us to be.

Here are some basic roles we need to provide to the students entrusted to our care. In our Barefoot Training module called "Engage," we talk about three defined roles: advisor, advocate, and guide. These concepts have been developed by Chris Folmsbee, who has helped frame in a simple way what roles we need to take on in youth ministry.

The Youth Worker as an Advisor

Students are dying for an adult who can look at them and help them understand how to make decisions that will affect their lives. This isn't about making decisions *for* your students but rather allowing them to enter in the process of learning how to make good decisions.

Students need an adult who will be there no matter what time it is or what has happened because of the choices they have made. Just like a financial advisor can't make you invest your money in a certain money-market fund, you as an advisor in youth ministry can't make a student do a certain thing.

An advisor asks good questions and allows students to be in a safe place in which to process the answers to those questions. Students need to learn how to wrestle through decisions for themselves as they move from adolescence to adulthood.

≡ **Where could you develop the role of an advisor in your youth ministry and life?**

≣ **Who currently acts as an advisor in your youth ministry?**

≣ **Whom do you need to come alongside of and be an advisor to?**

The Youth Worker as a Guide

I had the privilege of climbing a mountain the first year I was in college in Colorado. We spent an entire day climbing a 14,500-foot mountain near Estes Park. We needed a guide who would tell us where to put our feet, how to lean into the mountain, and really how to survive climbing this mountain. The view from the top was spectacular. It was great to make it on top of that mountain, but we needed the guide to get us there.

Students need adults in their lives who give them enormous amounts of encouragement and remind them that they can make it in life. They need adults who remind them of the promises found in Jeremiah 29:11-13—that God has a great plan and purpose for them.

It doesn't stop at encouragement, though. Students need to be empowered to do the things God is calling them to be a part of. The era of waiting for students to hit a magical age to finally be able to do what God has laid on their hearts needs to disappear.

Empowerment in youth ministry needs to have a tangible resource attached to it where it isn't about youth workers getting the praise for what we have done but rather a focused effort to resource the dreams, visions, and hopes of the students in our care as they invite the kingdom of God to be here now.

≣ **Where could you develop the role of a guide in your youth ministry and life?**

≣ **Who currently acts as a guide in your youth ministry?**

≣ **Whom do you need to come alongside of and be a guide to in your youth ministry?**

The Youth Worker as an Advocate

The majority of us in youth ministry would have no struggle with the roles of advisor or guide for students, but many of us have never thought through what it means to be a student's advocate.

Students are marginalized by the world in which they live. People usually think the worst of them before they think anything positive. In reality, this hasn't changed from the time that many of us grew up in environments where we were told to sit there and be quiet.

One of the greatest gifts you can bless a student with is being their advocate and simply giving them a voice. Advocacy for students can look like stepping in for them and helping them communicate the injustice that is happening to them. It can be support for them when they are having relational struggles. Or it can simply be lifting students up to their rightful place.

Jesus was an advocate for the disciples by calling them to be part of something they didn't deserve to be part of and then by proclaiming that powerful promise over them in John 14:12, which says that they will do even greater things than he has done.

≡ **Where could you develop the role of an advocate in your youth ministry and life?**

≡ **Who currently acts as an advocate in your youth ministry?**

≡ **Whom do you need to come alongside of and be an advocate for?**

———

There is a variety of topics to teach your students as you work hard to share the entire redemptive story of God with them. Each of us has unique challenges and contextual differences, but I want to encourage you to look at the time you have with your students each week and organize your curriculum or teaching efforts into two broad headings. We have the opportunity to impact our students' spiritual well-being as well as help them develop their life skills.

Spiritual Teaching

There are a lot of great people and resources out there to help you disciple your students to live like Jesus. I encourage you to help your students understand the entire story of God and what God calls them to in the pages of his Word.

Students who fall in love with God from the pages of his Word have a great chance of staying firm when they leave our youth ministry settings. Teach your students how to fall in love with Jesus as they watch you live out what it means to truly love the Father.

Be transparent and interactive. Let students see your doubts, your shortcomings, and the times when you truly are in the center of God's will. Let your life teach more strongly than words and always let students into your heart—the good and bad. Teach the way Jesus did, by simply taking the everyday events of this world, with all the pain and struggle, and redeeming them for good!

≡ What are you currently teaching your students in word and in action?

≡ Where can you let students experience the honesty of your Christian walk?

Life-Skill Teaching

Youth ministries focus large portions of their efforts on equipping students spiritually, which should be the priority. Let me push you a little, however, to consider the idea that, if youth ministry only equips spiritually, they are developing people who will struggle in the world in which we live.

Jesus was incredible at bridging spiritual lessons for the disciples with life lessons or skills that the disciples would need to have developed to make it after he left. These lessons ranged from paying taxes to Caesar to what to do if someone didn't accept the message to how to make preparations for an event. These were critical lessons for the disciples as they planted the early church after Christ left.

Today's youth ministries need to learn how to teach students a variety of subjects, such as how to resolve conflict, how to build relationships, what clothes to wear or not wear, how to cook healthy meals, and why you don't steal music.

Yes, all of these can be taught from a spiritual dynamic, but I encourage you to teach these without bringing in spiritual lessons. Allow students to make the spiritual connection themselves rather than unintentionally leading them to feel like Christianity is a bunch of rules.

≡ **What do you need to teach your students in regards to life skills?**

≡ **How can you teach it without necessarily attaching a spiritual lesson to it?**

———

Students are why we do youth ministry. The thrill and agony of watching them succeed and fail are part of the journey of youth ministry. At the end of the day, we love students, and it doesn't make sense to everyone, but those of us who are in it get it. The greatest gift you can give to your students is allowing them to watch your life and find that being a Christ follower works in this world, that it makes sense, and that it is the best decision they can make.

Prayer*

I have revealed you to those whom you gave me out of the world. They were yours; you gave them to me and they have obeyed your word. Now they know that everything you have given me comes from you. For I gave them the words you gave me and they accepted them. They knew with certainty that I came from you, and they believed that you sent me. I pray for them. I am not praying for the world, but for those you have given me, for they are yours. All I have is yours, and all you have is mine. And glory has come to me through them. I will remain in the world no longer, but they are still in the world, and I am coming to you. Holy Father, protect them by the power of your name—the name you gave me—so that they may be one as we are one. While I was with them, I protected them and kept them safe by that name you gave me. None has been lost except the one doomed to destruction so that Scripture would be fulfilled. I am coming to you now, but I say these things while I am still in the world, so that they may have the full measure of my joy within them. I have given them your word and the world has hated them, for they are not of the world any more than I am of the world. My prayer is not that you take them out of the world but that you protect them from the evil one. They are not of the world, even as I am not of it. Sanctify them by the truth; your word is truth. As you sent me into the world, I have sent them into the world. For them I sanctify myself, that they too may be truly sanctified.

*John 17:6-19

SEVEN

PARENTS

This chapter would have been very different if I had written it before I had children. I am one of those people now. You know the person the youth pastor struggles with. I am a parent of a junior high student. I know what it feels like. It is now you against me, and you dread the phone call or email from me.

Yes, I am a parent of a junior high girl turning into a young woman, and I expect you to be everything and more for my daughter. I expect you to be her activity planner and keep her amused every weekend. I expect you to be her spiritual guide and convince her that a life with Christ is the only way to go. I have a *list* of expectations if you want me to share them with you. Let's be honest—I want you to have fear when you see me walking toward you.

In all seriousness, I am finally a parent of a junior high girl, and my wife and I have been praying for you for many years. My prayer has been that we would be a support for you as you help our daughter find that a life with Christ is truly the most important thing she can give her life to. I have waited for this day, and I am thrilled that you and your team will be speaking into the life of my daughter.

For many years, I was the youth pastor who struggled to juggle all those parental demands, whether they were verbalized or merely perceived. I remember wishing and longing for a relationship with parents that wasn't dependent on what my end product was or whether their kids went home happy at the end of the night.

As we work with students, it shouldn't ever be us versus them, but so often that is where things end up. This isn't healthy for the student, the parent, or the youth worker. This tendency must change because, to be honest, I need you to speak to my young daughters in a way that my wife and I won't be able to.

As with all ministry environments and relationships, it is important for us to understand the context. The current generation of parents is the first group of people who have personal youth ministry experience. Many of these parents attended youth ministry during the time it went from a volunteer-led Sunday-school-style program to a paid, full-time youth pastor with youth group activities showing up on the calendar.

These parents fondly remember their former youth ministry experience, which was built on some flawed foundations. Youth ministry of the past had as one of its goals to keep kids safe and busy at the church. It was created to give kids a healthy alternative to what was going on in the world.

This set of parents will remember youth ministry consisting of a midweek Bible Study, regular events, and weekly Sunday school. They will remember it as a fond time of their lives, and they will desire this for their children. It was great experience for them because it relationally connected them to the church in a way that didn't involve just sitting in a pew like they were accustomed to.

Be prepared for some discussions with parents that revolve around where youth ministry has come from and where it is today. Invest time in understanding their past youth ministry experience, and encourage them in the new foundations of youth ministry. It is important for us to find common ground with parents of students where we can mutually understand each other's ministry contexts.

———

Everyone has needs, no matter how rich they are, how well organized, or how relationally connected they might be. The parents in your youth ministry have needs that many of them actually want help meeting, but they are afraid to ask because they are overly concerned with their teenagers making it. Parents have needs you can meet even though you might be a young youth pastor who doesn't have children and may not even be married. Parents trust you, and usually this is evident in the high expectations they have of you.

Need for Friendship

One of the goals of youth ministry is to connect students relationally so they feel like they belong and can share the stories of their lives. In the same way we do this for students, we need to provide this connecting point for parents.

The reality is that the older adults become (combined with having children), the less time they have and the less effort they put into building relationships with one another. Their time and effort are spent shuttling their children to activities, keeping up on homework, and managing full-time jobs.

One of the ways youth ministry can break down the barriers with parents is simply to provide relational connection points for parents so together they can share the struggles, frustrations, and concerns they all have. This in turn provides you and your youth ministry team the chance to build friendships away from the demands of life. I encourage you to constantly be looking at how to connect parents.

Need for Affirmation

We all need to feel affirmed, noticed, and thanked. Unfortunately, this doesn't happen regularly enough. Speaking from experience, being the parent of a teenager can be a thankless job.

When I talk about a parent's need for affirmation, I want you to think of affirmation in a different way from just affirming parenting technique. One of the strongest ways we can affirm parents in our youth ministry is to tell them something great that their children did away from their care. When you take the time to compliment their children, you remind parents that their children are learning the things they are so desperately trying to teach them at home. Essentially, you are affirming their parental role.

Need for Assistance

A time will come for every parent when they will need help in parenting. There is a range of situations or needs that will come into the life of a student that will require their parents to need the assistance of a larger group of people. A youth ministry that has success with parents is one that comes alongside parents, taking on the role of a respite worker who provides short-term help or relief from a problem.

Assistance can come in many different forms, from providing parental resources to providing mediation or simply a safe place for students to recalibrate who they are. If your youth ministry is viewed as a safe refuge for parents and their children, then parents will have no problem asking for assistance from you and your team and, in turn, supporting your ministry.

≣ **What needs have parents in your youth ministry expressed to you or your team?**

≣ **What are some creative ways for you to come alongside the parents in your youth ministry?**

Every parent-child relationship is unique. There are challenges each parent and student face that can't be solved by one simple program the youth ministry might or might not offer. I am scared for my daughter as she moves from being a cute baby who is learning how to speak the language all around her into a beautiful young woman of God. There are things Michelle and I have prayed for for our daughters ever since they became a part of our lives. Let me share with you four things that as a parent I would love for my daughter's youth pastor, youth workers, and youth ministry to do:

Honor my Family

I know my family has quirks and at times isn't committed to your greatest plans, but honor us a family unit. Help me learn how to navigate the crazy teenage years that are ahead of me, and help me learn how to connect with my daughter in a spiritual way. Honor my family by not competing with our family times and having a calendar so full of activities that we can't spend time growing together as a family.

Communicate with Us

Learn how to communicate with me in a way that will make me feel valued and informed. Don't just go with the easiest and most convenient way for you to get something off your desk. Ask me how I want you to communicate with me because, at the end of the day, I want to have a relationship with you that is deeper than the weekly email blast. I want my child to be involved with you, but I need you to help me understand why you do the things you do. Speak to me in a way that allows me to understand your heart, not just the program details. I want my child to find friendship with Jesus and with other students.

Facilitate Relationships with Other Parents

I am so concerned with my daughter's development in all aspects of life that my family's world revolves around her. We run her to everything, and we have sacrificed our own relationships with peers so we can help our daughter make it. Help my wife and me build relationships with other parents who struggle with the same things we do. Help us build a relationship with you so we can assist you when our daughter is at home with us. We want to feel part of something bigger than our little family's home and world.

Be Intentional about Volunteers

My daughter longs for an adult woman she can look up to and see Jesus at work in. Don't recruit people out of need; recruit out of passion. Allow my daughter to see a volunteer who loves her and wants to show her that this life Christ calls us to is an adventure. My daughter wants to see someone other than her mom and dad fall madly in love with Jesus. Recruit the best team you can find of people who are crazy for the students and madly in love with God. Please don't have a volunteer serving with you who doesn't want to be there because my daughter will sniff it out.

Don't be scared of us parents. We have been praying for you as long as we have had our children. Be *our* pastor too. We need you to help us allow our children to be all that God has created them to be. Enter into a relationship with us where you can speak into our lives and we can speak into yours. At the end of the day, we all have the same end goal in mind. We are on the same team.

Prayer*

O merciful Lord God, thou hast commanded and enjoined me to honor my father and mother, and thou thyself hast shown even until death humble obedience to thy Father. From the depth of my soul I fervently beseech thee, O gracious Jesus Christ, my God, hear my prayer and have mercy upon my parents, who have given birth to me and are bringing me up in thy grace and love. Protect them from all evil, harm and sickness; grant them health, and mercifully pour forth thy bountiful blessings upon them. Bless their efforts and deeds; have mercy on them according to thy great mercy, that faithfully serving thee, through them I also may be worthy to praise and serve thee. Amen.

*An Orthodox Prayer

EIGHT

VOLUNTEERS

You need great volunteers to have a great youth ministry. The depth of your students will be directly proportional to the quality of your volunteers. The consistency of your volunteers will be directly proportional to the consistency of care for your students. The list could go on and on.

Your volunteers aren't crowd control. Nor are they people you can count toward insurance compliance. They aren't people who do the things you don't want to do. Volunteers have the ability to impact students in a way you aren't able to. They show students that serving God is a natural part of life. They show students the value of contributing to something bigger than the concerns of their own lives.

Unfortunately, we often recruit people out of desperation rather than passion. We have our roster filled out, and every year people give the one-year commitment, often never to be seen again.

One of the most important ways we can care for our students is to care for our volunteers. Our volunteer team really is an extension of ourselves. I used to complain about how much work I had to do until I began to think through the commitment it takes to be a youth volunteer. A youth volunteer gives up weeknights and weekends to love on students. They often have other jobs, and yet they give up holiday time to come and serve alongside students on mission trips. They open up their wallets to simply serve because they love students. Youth volunteers are some of the most sacrificial people I know.

77
*

When I came to Grace Baptist Church in the fall of 1994, the team was tired and ready for a youth pastor. I met a few of the core volunteers and began the process of casting a new vision for what I thought youth ministry was supposed to be at Grace Baptist Church.

After a year of finding my way and speaking into the lives of the five junior high students and seven senior high students God gave me, I began to build my team. I simply committed to casting the vision of what the student ministry could become if God blessed us and showed favor on our efforts. That year, we went from a handful of volunteers to twenty-two adults who were passionate about the possibility of life change happening with students. The only problem was that we only had fourteen students. We were discouraged as a team and trying to figure out why God brought so many adult volunteers if we didn't have very many students.

God taught me an important lesson that year about stewardship. Stewardship is so often taught with a financial focus, but there are many stewardship principles that involve people. The principle God wanted me to learn was that he would only trust me with the number of students I would be a good steward with. This principle shaped the years to come with our youth staff and youth volunteers as we worked to show God that we would be good stewards with all the students he entrusted to our care. As we went through that year, there was a belief that God was up to something bigger than what we could see with our own eyes. I could sense it, and my systematic mind was already creating flow charts so every student would be cared for.

Then the worst happened. As we sat in a youth staff meeting at a volunteer's house in Kensington, the youth volunteers looked at me and said, "We are doing youth ministry wrong." It wasn't only one of them saying it; it was the entire team. It crushed me, and I thought, *Who needs these dumb volunteers anyway?*

But my team of volunteers wasn't making a judgment on me as a professional youth worker. They were just so passionate about students that God had been speaking to their hearts before he had spoken to mine. My team felt so confident in all of our relationships that they were able to be honest and share with me their opinions about youth ministry, even though they knew it could offend me. I believe God blessed our youth ministry because of that moment.

Many of those original volunteers continued to serve in the youth ministry for as long as God called me to work at Grace Baptist Church. I care deeply for them and miss those times of ministering together as a team.

So, how do you actually get people to join you on this journey of youth ministry, or better yet, why do they give their lives alongside you for students?

Recruit According to Passion

Everyone is passionate about something, and when people are passionate about something, they are willing to give up their time and their money. So often in youth ministry, we recruit to fill a certain number of positions rather than allowing passion to dictate the vision.

Relationships are strengthened between each other because joy is always a product of passion. The key to deep relationships with our youth volunteers is directly attached to the ability we have to resource people's passions.

Some of my most enjoyable times in ministry have been when I watched people serve in their passions because that is how God has wired them to be. People's whose hearts are open for students and are not limited by the program of youth ministry have had the most impact on the lives of the students.

> What are some passions you have heard from your youth volunteers that you could possibly look at resourcing and accomplishing?

Recruit According to Gifting

God makes it very clear that each one of us has a contribution and each one has at least one spiritual gift. It is important for us to create opportunities for people in the church, regardless of age, to use their gifts (both earthly abilities and spiritual gifts) in our youth ministries.

As people begin to serve and find fulfillment in their contribution to students, relationships begin to develop in a deep way because of our realization of how God's economy of workers works. God takes our feeble efforts as individuals and turns these efforts into the supernatural as we truly form the body of Christ.

It is so easy for us to find youth volunteers who are all cut from the same mold. They talk a certain way, can play the games we demand them to play, and are all a certain age. But one of the most powerful illustrations of community is when we truly reflect the body of our church within our ministry.

People need to find a place in your youth ministry where they can use the uniqueness of how God has created them, whether by using administrative gifts, praying for students, or running a game. Strive in your youth ministries to include an accurate representation of the gifts so students can see how they personally can make a contribution to God's kingdom by watching your volunteers.

≡ **How can you broaden your youth volunteer team by recruiting different abilities and spiritual gifts?**

Recruit According to Community

It is important to realize that one of the most compelling reasons people will have to join your youth ministry team is to be part of something larger than themselves. People might have a growing passion for students or even feel like they have to serve somewhere in the church because of a message they have just heard. The key to keeping these volunteers is to develop a community that loves and cares for each other outside the walls of the church building or the duty of serving.

There were many times, when I had a team of almost fifty volunteers, that I had to remind them that the youth gatherings were about the students and not them hanging out. They had developed such deep relationships that they truly enjoyed being with one another.

One of the keys to developing an effective volunteer team that cares for youth is to develop community amongst your volunteers in the same way in which we develop community for students. Make it a priority and use the time and resources to develop lifelong friendships with people who want to belong.

Think of creative ways to develop community with your youth volunteers. This can involve going away on retreats as youth volunteers or simply grabbing a late-night snack at the end of a youth activity. Make sure to raise this priority in your youth ministry so volunteers will *want* to stick around in your youth ministry rather than view their service as the fulfillment of a short-term obligation.

☰ **How can you increase the level of community that is shared with your youth volunteers?**

───

It is sad in the church environment that we don't value volunteers the way we really should. Volunteers are viewed as a necessary means to get us to the goal we have developed for our ministry. We value them as an afterthought when we throw together a last-minute banquet or send out a form letter, thanking everyone for their contributions.

Volunteers sometimes are viewed as crowd control, extra hands for games, small-group facilitators, or just people who help us meet the requirements of the protection policies our insurance companies demand. If we valued our volunteers and truly worked to understand the sacrifices they make, we would have less of a volunteer crisis in our churches.

As I have moved from the paid leadership role of youth ministry to a volunteer role, I have learned a few lessons about what I want from the youth pastor I serve alongside.

Be My Pastor

Volunteers long for you to enter into a friendship that supersedes their weekly service, but they also long for you to be their pastor. As a pastor, you have a great privilege to be there when pain affects their families or when they need someone to help them work through a crisis. They want you to lead them spiritually and be the hands and feet of Jesus in a practical, life-giving way.

≡ What are some ways you can be a pastor to your youth volunteers?

Be My Teacher

Youth ministry is an ever-changing environment that youth volunteers need to be equipped to work in. One valuable and ongoing training tool is the ability for volunteers to be taught by watching you. Let them into your life away from the white board and PowerPoint. Move teaching away from the stale environment of round tables, and allow the team to serve together, observing and learning from one other. Teach volunteers your *values* for student ministry, rather than just doing a seminar.

≡ What are some creative ways you can teach your youth volunteers about the values of youth ministry?

Appreciate Me

Youth pastors work incredibly hard and are not often noticed for their work. So often, our frustrations with how we are valued in the church are brought into the group of volunteers we work with. No matter what job we do in life, we always want to be noticed for our efforts. Find ways to add value to a volunteer's life. Think of different ways you can validate the volunteer and acknowledge their sacrifices for the youth ministry. Surprise your volunteers with small personal tokens of your appreciation. Notice what they do and keep them focused on things you see them serving with joy in.

≡ What are some ways you can love, appreciate, and value the youth volunteers on your team?

———

A student called my house late one evening, and instantly I knew something wasn't right. He said he needed help, and I quickly put on my ambulance driver's hat. I simply told this student I was there to help him.

The student responded, "I don't need *your* help, Pastor Matt. I need you to give me my small-group leader's phone number." At that moment, he needed his small-group leader and not me, and that was a great thing.

One of the greatest joys I have experienced in my years of youth ministry was working alongside that group of youth volunteers at Grace Baptist Church. These were people who saw me grow up and allowed me to make more mistakes than I should have been allowed to make. They sacrificed enormous amounts of time, holidays, and money to serve the hundreds of students who came through the ministry at Grace Baptist Church.

They were innovators in many ways in regards to the spiritual formation of students in Calgary. When we didn't have enough money for mission trips or when our student ministries budget was maxed out, they sacrificed their own money because they believed in the students and in me. One of the things I miss most about not being a full-time, paid youth pastor is my volunteer team.

Appreciate them; cultivate them; equip them; and they'll serve well.

Prayer

God, thank you for the adults who serve alongside me to speak into the lives of students. May you redeem their time and sacrifices in a way that you only can. Allow them to feel fulfilled for their sacrifices and find great success in serving you. Develop within them your heart for their students as they spiritually develop these students. May these students see Jesus alive and well in their lives.

83
*

NINE

INTERNS

One of the most exciting aspects of youth ministry is getting the chance to develop the next generation of ministry workers for the greater church world. We walk alongside students who, while under our tutelage, are called into full-time missions. Other students feel the call to be youth pastors or children's pastors then end up coming back to work alongside us in an internship.

The dictionary defines an internship as "any official or formal program to provide practical experience for beginners in an occupation or profession." In the ministry world, we probably define internships as "the ability to get cheap help."

In all seriousness, many churches consider interns merely to be a cheap workforce who will hopefully learn some practical skills. Interns come into our youth ministries in different stages of life, and our duty is to develop them holistically to face the challenges that will arise in youth ministry.

Youth ministries (and churches in general) need to take the time to develop an internship strategy that accomplishes foundational ministry principles for the student. It is important for interns to have opportunities to explore their ministry calls in the context of real-life, practical ministry. Interns need to understand the rhythms of youth ministry and the toll ministry will take on both individuals and their families. Finally, interns need to experience the joys and heartbreaks that naturally come when we work with broken people. A comprehensive internship will provide a student the head start to develop the skills needed for ministry.

An Intern Needs Mentoring

As I look back on my life now that I am heading toward forty years old, I realize I would have a hard time counting on more than one hand the number of times I have been mentored. In my own life, I have a deep desire to be mentored in principles of life and ministry.

Most times, interns come into our ministries with all kinds of preconceived notions of grandeur and raw thoughts of being able to do ministry better than we could ever do it. Usually, they have been taught in the unrealistic laboratory of the classroom, but even so, they come wanting to gain and feel our approval.

An effective intern relationship is one that involves a strategic development plan for interns in all aspects of life. Spend time helping them develop their relational abilities with friends and their spouses if they are married. Invest time in getting to know them outside the walls of the church and speak into their lives there. Focus on the whole being before simply equipping them to do the work of the ministry.

A good intern relationship is one that goes beyond the internship period, into a lifelong relationship of mutual trust and support. As a supervisor of interns, you aren't just signing a form making sure they complete the tasks of ministry; you are developing them to make it in ministry for the long term.

≡ How can you transition your internship relationships to be mentoring relationships?

An Intern Needs Empowerment

The depth of a relationship is often dependent on the amount of empowerment we feel from the relationship. Empowerment comes naturally as a relationship develops, but with interns, we need to empower earlier on in the relationship. Empowerment means, *I value your contribution, and I believe you have the ability to do this.*

Empowerment will cost you, and there will be times you will regret that you allowed an intern to make a decision or allowed one to fail to follow through on a commitment. All of those struggles are a natural part of a protected internship relationship that can be both rewarding and frustrating at the same time.

Youth ministry, as it moves into the future, needs to learn the art of empowerment as a whole. If we teach interns how to be empowered in their jobs, it will be a natural part of their future ministries.

≡ **How can you empower your interns to feel like they are valued in your youth ministry?**

An Intern Needs Trust

It is easy to evaluate trust in a relationship by merely assigning a job to be completed. It can be simply the words, "I trust you to complete the task," but in an internship relationship it can also be so much more. Interns hear your frustrations in ministry and learn how to deal with those in constructive ways. Interns enter into the pain of relationships that have been fractured because of the hurt and brokenness that can come in ministry. Interns are set up for failure when they only see the joys of ministry, void of its pain.

An intern relationship that is limited to simply doing tasks and jobs sets the student up for a long and lonely ministry experience. Some of my deepest conversations with interns came in the unfiltered and raw moments of doing ministry with them. Interns value the trust that is shared by adults in their lives.

≡ **How can you increase the trust both professionally and relationally with your interns?**

An Intern Needs Exposure

Relationships are strengthened with interns when we allow them into different aspects of the ministry. Unfortunately, most youth pastors don't stay in youth ministry for life, so there is an enormous benefit in allowing interns to see different aspects of the ministry of the church.

Allow them to serve in children's ministry and spend time with the senior pastor, going on hospital visits or preparing for a sermon. Let interns go to the seniors' luncheon and share their testimonies, or even let them go to ministries outside the walls of the church to open up their global views of ministry. It is important for interns to learn the scope of ministry inside and outside the church so they are aware of the opportunities they have to contribute to God's kingdom.

Make sure to allow them to also be involved in the areas that are naturally your areas of passion and abilities. Let them find success in areas you might really enjoy ministering in and want to continue to do. A goal of an internship is to allow students to have a holistic understanding of the ministry. Make sure to affirm them in public for the contributions they have made to the ministry and the team.

≡ **Where do you need to allow your interns to gain exposure in the ministry?**

≡ **How can you prepare your interns for the realities of ministry?**

———

An internship can be both a valuable and frustrating experience as you have a variety of students come and share in the work of ministry. Internships are important experiences for students as they learn the many inner workings of the church and how to navigate the struggles of ministry. Allowing students to intern within the framework of your ministry gives them a chance to discover their call in a safe and protected environment. Let them see you be in love with Jesus.

Prayer*

Give me, O Lord, I pray thee: firm faith, unwavering hope, perfect charity.

Pour into my heart the Spirit of wisdom and understanding,

the Spirit of counsel and spiritual strength,

the Spirit of knowledge and true godliness,

and the Spirit of Thy holy fear.

Light eternal, shine in my heart.

Power eternal, deliver me from evil.

Wisdom eternal, scatter the darkness of my ignorance.

Might eternal, pity me.

Grant that I may ever seek thy face with all my heart and soul and strength;

and, in thine infinite mercy, bring me at last to thy holy presence,

where I shall behold Thy glory and possess thy promised joys.

89
*

---

*St. Alcuin of York (735-804)

TEN

CONGREGATION

It has been said that church would be a lot easier if it didn't involve people or simply had people who were just the same as us. The reality is that this is not possible and does not describe what the church is intended to be.

So often as youth workers, we struggle with our role in the big church. If we are on a smaller team, we can be viewed as the pastor-in-waiting or training for the big time, while, if we are on a larger team, we can be viewed as the kid who hangs out with the kids.

Either way, receiving credibility from the congregation usually doesn't come from our title or position in the church, as it can for many other staff members. The children's ministry pastor may get accolades from baby dedications or young children accepting Jesus into their hearts. The associate pastor may get recognition for their Sunday school or small-group ministries while the youth ministry leader often inherits the negative comments because they have put more holes in the wall or used the hand-bell mats as a wrestling ring.

Although the congregation may make some negative comments toward the youth ministry that aren't warranted, many times, youth ministry volunteers and professionals contribute to the misconceptions about what really goes on behind the walls of youth ministry.

The students we serve usually don't look like the perfect kids on baby dedication Sundays. They start to come with some baggage that is not so easily hidden from the congregation. Maybe it is the cigarette can outside the front doors of the church on youth ministry night or the music our students respond to or simply the confusion students bring to adults because they don't fit a nice and perfect mold.

Let's be honest here. There is no coincidence that youth ministry happens on nights when nothing else is happening in the church. We slot our youth ministry programs into Tuesday or Thursday nights, when no one uses the church, sheltering the congregation from some of the things that happen in youth ministry. But God has orchestrated the exact people within the walls of the church to be the ones called to help and support you. One of the areas we youth pastors and volunteers don't do a great job in is partnering with the congregation God has given to us.

Your congregation has been sent by God to provide you with many of the resources you lack in youth ministry. Many times, the issue is with us constructing fortresses around our youth ministries that let no one see what is really happening. We need to move away from viewing the congregation as the enemy and cease trying to protect youth ministry from perceived dangers that aren't really there.

Youth ministry needs to open up the doors and allow people entrance to be a part of the development of the future generation that will hopefully change the world and the church.

When Paul writes those familiar words in 1 Corinthians 12, he describes the many different parts that make up the body of Christ or simply the church. So often, I looked at those verses through the lens of the recruitment of my volunteer team. *I need this team member to do this, and I am missing this person with this gift mix.* In retrospect, I believe God provides the congregation as the greater tool for us to accomplish what we believe God has called our youth ministries to.

I want to encourage you to look at your ministry through the eyes of your congregation. Are they seeing where they can contribute to your ministry? Where are they able to be a part of the youth ministry?

Let me share a few thoughts from my experience on how a youth ministry can involve a congregation in a deeper and more fruitful manner.

Clear Vision

So often with the whole church congregation, youth ministry is speaking a totally different language. Youth ministry has a different (or we may think a cooler) name than the rest of the church. Youth ministry often operates with a different set of values than the church does and even gets into discussions about how they are doing things better than the rest of the church.

Relational fractures often appear not only within the different ministries of the church but throughout the congregation as a whole. Youth ministry takes on the role of being the rebel while the congregation struggles to see how it coincides with the youth ministry.

Seniors in the congregation wonder why the big youth crusades have left or why there isn't Sunday school anymore. Instead of bringing clarity to these issues, youth ministry begins to wear proudly a badge of honor for being different from the rest. Unfortunately this can lead to alienating the masses who long to be part of the youth ministry.

One of the ways youth ministry can come alongside the church's congregation is to be clear with vision and purpose. Every time the youth ministry has the privilege of sharing from the front of the church, it is imperative that you share stories that point people to how you are accomplishing the student ministry's vision. Don't use fancy taglines or coded messages that get lost in translation. Simply speak in concise, clear, and understandable terms that make sense to them as a congregation.

One of the greatest abilities Jesus had while he was on earth was to speak in a language that different groups of people could understand. He constantly spoke words that reflected his vision and purpose. Whether it was the religious leaders asking him a question or a group of farmers he was telling a story to, he spoke in ways they could understand.

Youth ministry needs to use a similar posture to the one Jesus took. When we are meeting with seniors, we need to use simple terms such as *evangelism* and *discipleship*, rather than using our catch phrases that only people in youth ministry understand. The clearer we are, the more people feel that they can contribute to the greater good of our youth ministry.

≡ What messaging have you been providing to your church in regard to the youth ministry and where it is headed?

≡ What would your congregation understand as to why youth ministry exists in your church?

≡ What terminology have you been using that has brought possible confusion to people groups in your church?

≡ What people groups do you need to meet with to allow them to understand pieces of your youth ministry?

Two-Way Partnership

So often in life and in youth ministry we want it to be all about us. I found myself complaining about how our youth ministry didn't get all the new stuff that the other ministries got. It was easy to pile on with congregational members about how neglected youth ministry was in regard to the resources we were given (or not given). In retrospect, I took on the dynamic of the younger brother in the story of the prodigal son in Luke 15. I am pretty sure I turned people away from youth ministry simply because of my bellyaching about the perceived misfortunes of my youth ministry.

I complained about the budget. I complained when we were asked to set up a room or serve at a banquet. I even complained for the sake of complaining. Rather than looking at those opportunities as places to partner with others and broaden the stretch of our youth ministry, I became toxic.

A healthy youth ministry is one that partners with other ministries and members of the congregation. A healthy youth ministry is always looking for potential in each congregational member. Searching out their passions and calls that will strengthen the bond between congregational members and allowing them to see that we aren't just obsessed about our own deal. A youth ministry that is able to partner both within and outside its own walls allows people the ability to see that the youth ministry is passionate about the whole kingdom of God. A youth ministry that is willing to partner shares the resources God has blessed the church with as a whole.

There are many resources that God has blessed your youth ministry with. This can be anything from specifically skilled people on your team to physical equipment that you have or even connections you have with people. A youth ministry that is effective is willing to share with others to see them succeed.

≣ How are you partnering with others outside of the walls of your youth ministry?

≣ How would your students describe partnership with other people inside and outside the church?

≣ What resources do you have that you are willing to share?

Open Door

95
*

A youth ministry that is effective in being a healthy member of the congregation is one that is wide open for people to contribute to. So often, youth ministries become closed off to the rest of the church as we seek comfort in the solace that we can protect ourselves from others simply by hiding in our caves called youth ministry. But to bring about deep relationships outside the walls of youth ministry, we must allow people to naturally connect *within* the walls of the youth ministry.

Allow people to check out your youth ministry by observing during your gathering times. Ask people to come and cook or drive a van or simply to come and help with check in. The more youth ministry is seen as open and accepting, the more likely it is that the congregation will view youth ministry as a place they can serve.

When you open the doors to your youth ministry, you allow people the chance to fall in love with what is going on in your ministry. The congregation wants to pray and fall in love with what the next generation is, and unfortunately, they see a foggy picture because of the fortresses we've built.

≡ **Would people perceive your youth ministry as an open ministry or a closed ministry?**

≡ **What positive attributes of your youth ministry are you hiding from people in your church? Are there any negatives ones that you are hiding from people?**

≡ **How easy is it for people to check out your youth ministry?**

Hope for the Future

One of the greatest things youth ministry can provide to the congregation is hope for the future. Most seniors in the church long for the chance to see that the church they helped build will continue into the future. One of the greatest gifts a youth ministry can provide the seniors is the assurance ministry will continue after they are gone.

In youth ministry we often fail to provide hope to the generations who have come before because we are intimidated or threatened by them. We need to allow them to see that we are passionate about the same things they are and care deeply about them too.

Bless people in the congregation by giving them real-life examples of students and stories from your youth ministry that give them hope. Allow them to interact with students who understand where God is calling them. Forging these relationships will help your congregation understand that the future looks bright.

≡ **What specific people in your church do you need to get your students to interact with?**

☰ How is your student ministry giving a hope for the future to your church?

———

Read 1 Corinthians 12 out of *The Message*. Evaluate this against your relationship with your congregation.

Just as a body, though one, has many parts, but all its many parts form one body, so it is with Christ. For we were all baptized by one Spirit so as to form one body—whether Jews or Gentiles, slave or free—and we were all given the one Spirit to drink. Even so the body is not made up of one part but of many. Now if the foot should say, "Because I am not a hand, I do not belong to the body," it would not for that reason stop being part of the body. And if the ear should say, "Because I am not an eye, I do not belong to the body," it would not for that reason stop being part of the body. If the whole body were an eye, where would the sense of hearing be? If the whole body were an ear, where would the sense of smell be? But in fact God has placed the parts in the body, every one of them, just as he wanted them to be. If they were all one part, where would the body be? As it is, there are many parts, but one body. The eye cannot say to the hand, "I don't need you!" And the head cannot say to the feet, "I don't need you!" On the contrary, those parts of the body that seem to be weaker are indispensable, and the parts that we think are less honorable we treat with special honor. And the parts that are unpresentable are treated with special modesty, while our presentable parts need no special treatment. But God has put the body together, giving greater honor to the parts that lacked it, so that there should be no division in the body, but that its parts should have equal concern for each other. If one part suffers, every part suffers with it; if one part is honored, every part rejoices with it. Now you are the body of Christ, and each one of you is a part of it.

Prayer*

Lord, make this a generation of students who will revive the church and change the world.

———

*Borrowed from Pastor Dennis Gulley, who prays this every day

ELEVEN

FROM THE SENIOR PASTOR'S DESK

It happened when I least expected it. I remember stating clearly from behind a microphone numerous times throughout my tenure as a youth pastor that I would never, ever be a senior pastor. On youth pastor retreats, I used to make fun of them.

People in the church asked me when I was going to grow up and move into a real job or simply asked, "When will you use your gifts in the whole church?" Most times there was no malice behind their words, simply curiosity as they saw me mature in both my leadership and age.

I always answered that God had called me to work with students and that I hoped students would let me serve alongside them for many years to come. I loved students' passion and the ability they had to understand the truths of God. The thing I loved most was the challenge of moving a group of students together in such a way as to create a movement or something that truly was bigger than just the collection of individuals who make up a youth group.

Every year, I felt we had only discovered a piece of what God wanted for us. My office was strategically placed in the basement of the church, which was perfect for me. The church and its leadership respected what I did in youth ministry and were more than willing to share the success stories of what God was doing in youth ministry. It was all perfect in my own little world, and as a newly minted thirty-year-old, I thought, *This is the life.*

My church blessed me with a four-month sabbatical, and I settled in to the new routine of working to finish up my master's degree. Our church had entered into a building project, and instead of unifying the congregation, the opposite had happened, and disunity ran rampant. I met with the man who was my lead pastor at the time at a coffee shop in our community, and there he proclaimed dreadful words.

"For the benefit of my family, I am resigning from the church and have taken a church in Michigan."

Those words had a huge impact all by themselves because he and I had developed a deep working and personal relationship with each other. In my mind, I began to grieve the loss of my friend and boss. He wasn't finished, however, and I was brought back into the conversation when he uttered his next, potent words.

"I have recommended that you step in and lead the church for the next little while. You have the ability and are the best one to help this church through this tumultuous time." I felt anger in my heart and spirit and wondered why God would even consider letting this happen. The journey was about to begin as God began to do a work in my heart to restore some reconciliation and tear down some defenses I had built.

———

It was July 1 when I stepped into the role of the interim lead pastor. I thought that within six months, I would have proven I couldn't lead the church, and they would have given me back my real job. Even though I had two other full-time, paid staff members on my youth ministry team, I kept the title of youth pastor because I wasn't ready to give it up.

The first year found me deflecting full ownership of the lead pastor's role. I recognize this was simply a protectionist mechanism to hold onto the job I felt most comfortable in or had the most success in. Unfortunately, my selfishness created frustration for the youth ministry team and confusion for the church. I pleaded with God because I knew once I stepped fully into the lead pastor role, I would never be the youth pastor again.

As youth workers, our greatest success is when we develop students who share in the work of the ministry and can take the youth ministry to places beyond what we can. Just like David gave the temple plans to Solomon, so we in ministry need to create a culture of raising up our replacements, rather than selfishly clinging to ownership of our official titles of youth pastor.

———

I believed I had been a great associate staff member and was valuable to the team. I worked hard in my area and created a ministry the church could be proud of outside the walls of the church building. My contribution to the church had been to make youth ministry incredibly effective.

But as I began to lead the dreaded weekly staff meeting from the position of lead pastor, I realized what a poor team player I had developed into. As the youth pastor, I sat in those staff meetings biting my tongue so they would end quickly and I could go back to my work, which I felt was way more important than the business of the church.

As I stepped into the position of lead pastor, I was confronted with the realization that my silence and non-contribution in staff meetings had actually done more damage than good. If the whole church isn't healthy, then a youth ministry's façade of health will only be superficial. A youth ministry can't exist without the church as a whole. It doesn't matter how good a youth program is if the church isn't healthy. Our goal as youth ministry leaders needs to focus on the health of the church as a whole through the sharing of the resources we have in youth ministry.

———

When God speaks, we have no choice but to listen. It is never the listening I struggle with but rather the doing that tends to trip me up. As I stepped into the role of the lead pastor, God impressed upon my heart ten things the church needed to work through before the new lead pastor could come.

God made it clear to me that I was simply the transitional leader who would prepare the way for the new leader to be called. So often in the ministry environment we see issues but desire someone else to take care of the mess even though we know we should deal with it.

When the current leadership fails to deal with the issues and waits for the new leader to come, it slows down the process toward health. The new leader is forced to invest time in understanding the context of the problem before starting to deal with it.

In ministry, God calls us to be proactive when it comes to existent issues in the church. When transitions are imminent, it is important for leadership to commit to cleaning things up rather than expecting new leaders to focus their time working through these issues.

———

There were so many things I learned in my role as the lead pastor that I wish I had known as a youth pastor. The reality is that I would have had a different relationship with my senior pastors. I made so many incorrect assumptions about the role of a senior pastor that I wish I could go back and change.

As a youth worker, if you provide these few things to your senior pastor, not only will your relationship become stronger, but the church in return will become an effective bride of Christ.

#1: Relationship

A huge part of youth ministry is pursuit of relationships. One of the biggest realizations I had as I became the senior pastor was that almost every relationship a senior pastor has is not one of choice. Every other ministry in the church allows the individual in leadership to recruit their own teams, whereas senior pastors often do not get to choose the people they work with. At times, I found myself feeling very lonely.

The other aspect of relationship is that instantly the staff's perception of me changed. They acted similar to how I had by simply working in their own areas and doing what they got paid to do.

It is important as a member of a ministry staff for you to develop a trusting and honest relationship with your senior pastor. Allow him to find safety in his relationship with you and to be real with you.

#2: Support

In the culture in which we live, there are many things we say we support. We support sports teams when they are doing really well but lose interest when they are rebuilding. We support causes until the cause becomes too expensive or time consuming. It is one thing to say to your senior pastor that you support him and another thing to actually show support in action.

As I sat at the senior pastor's desk, wrestling through what bills should get paid when we didn't have enough money or how we would do the initiative God was leading us to do, I needed to have resources beyond what I had on my own. One of the greatest gifts you can bless your senior pastor with is the gift of the resources you have at your disposal in your ministry. Regularly ask your senior pastor what frustrations he has and see if your ministry has the resources to take them off his plate. Bless him by sharing your resources, and in return, later on down the road, he may be able to bless you by sharing his resources.

#3: Honor

Honor is defined simply as having high respect for someone, and this needs to be how you view your senior pastor. A senior pastor will never be perfect, but he has been called by God to lead the church and will be judged by God for what he did with that responsibility.

Over my years as a youth pastor, I believed I honored my senior pastor, but there were times and conversations I entered into when I wasn't honoring the man God had chosen for his church. People asked me my opinions about things as a youth pastor, and I devalued the leadership of the senior pastor by not throwing my support behind him.

Honor your senior pastor by always sharing with him personally about the struggles you might have with his leadership. Just as you long to have your senior pastor support you, support him first so he knows you are in his corner. The reality is that a senior pastor often feels like someone is coming over his shoulder, ready to attack him.

My time as the lead pastor at Grace Baptist Church was one of the greatest times in my life. It would have not been possible if it weren't for the many different groups of people who trusted me enough to let me lead them.

Just in case you were wondering, I still had my office in the basement and still wore a baseball cap to work more often than not. Probably the most important lesson I learned as a lead pastor was simply to never say "never" again.

Prayer*

Appreciate your pastoral leaders who gave you the Word of God. Take a good look at the way they live, and let their faithfulness instruct you, as well as their truthfulness.

---

* Hebrews 13:7, MSG

Cultivating Relationships outside the Church

Our relationships outside our own churches will be some of the most important ones we form as youth workers. However, relationships outside the church are usually an afterthought or something we do not necessarily get to in our week-to-week schedules.

Cultivating relationships outside the walls of the church building involves us placing a high priority on creating space in our calendars to allow these relationships to grow. As we develop these relationships, we are given the opportunity to put into practice what we continually ask our students to be and do.

OTHER MINISTRY COLLEAGUES

We all need people in our lives. It doesn't matter whether you are an introvert or an extrovert; you still need people. The difference is the amount of time we will spend with others. We were never meant to do ministry alone, but unfortunately many of us do.

I have been to my fair share of bad youth pastor networking meetings, where everyone brags (with exaggeration) about their ministry successes and advertise their next events. To be honest, I did my best to find as many excuses as I possibly could to stay away from networking meetings.

So, why is it important for us to have relationships with other ministry colleagues? Why should we create time in our lives to have relationships outside the walls of our churches?

Relationships outside the church walls are the fuel that allows us to recalibrate ourselves for the work of the ministry inside the church. There are many different types of relationships we can have with ministry colleagues, but let me give you a few you should look at having in your life.

More Experience

There are a few individuals in my life whom I respect deeply because they are further down the road then I have yet been. These individuals remind me that the problems and concerns I face are really small in the grand scheme of things. They have literally been there, done that, and survived it.

Seasoned veterans give you the ability to put your ministry in perspective. Usually these individuals have found a great balance in their lives, and just by spending a few hours with them every so often, you will feel encouraged and refreshed and find you are leaving with a right perspective. These individuals are never looking for attention and go about their work in a systematic yet strategic way. The wealth of wisdom they share is easily worth the cup of coffee it will cost you.

Different Philosophy

It is easy to get into a rut where we think, do, and act in the same ways we always have. We buy the same books, attend the same conferences, and pull the same file folders out each year to repeat the process again and again. This becomes more the case when we find ministry success and don't want to risk losing momentum.

But I have found the need to have people in my life with whom I don't always agree and those who do ministry completely differently from how I would. They think differently, talk differently, and act in a way that can even be uncomfortable for me at times, but they challenge me out of my ruts.

There are times when I have left meetings completely disagreeing (and even becoming agitated) about what they have said about ministry, but these types of people have pushed me to become better. The depth of relationship with these individuals has increased as we have learned to disagree with one another, but we love the same God, and we love students. Some of the most supportive people in my life have been these people who think differently than I do.

Young Perspective

It can be easy to judge ministry maturity by individuals' physical ages and write them off because of it. There were many times I walked into a room and felt people sizing me up based on my age. In ministry circles, we are usually drawn to people who are near our own ages and, because of this, we lose the perspective of young individuals who are not jaded in ministry.

It is critical for us to seek out relationships with people who are younger than ourselves and who have the ability to breathe excitement for ministry back into our lives. I don't believe it is any coincidence that Jesus recruited teenagers to be his disciples.

Make sure, though, that these relationships are mutual and don't default to internship kinds of relationships. Allow younger ministers to speak into your life, and be able to learn from individuals whom God has gifted and called to the work of ministry.

———

As I look back on my ministry career, these three types of relationships are the ones I have enjoyed outside the walls of the church that have helped me gain the right perspective on ministry. These relationships were there when I had to make decisions or when there were issues I needed outside opinions on from someone who wasn't in the situation.

≣ **Are there any people who are already in your life who fit these three categories?**

≣ **Who are some people you need to pursue relationships with?**

———

The relationships we build with other ministry colleagues will help us with longevity in our own ministry settings. They give us perspective and the ability to solve ministry issues as a team. God longs for us to function as a global team. There are some dynamics that occur when we truly develop relationships with other ministry colleagues. These understandings are actually the end products of these relationships.

Honesty

It is interesting to think that one of the areas many church leaders struggle with is honesty. We fudge our numbers to make ourselves look better; our stories become more dynamic as we change the facts just a little in the right direction; and we never really share with anyone the issues inside our ministries. Yet we call people to lives of honesty.

True relationships with other ministry colleagues force us to be honest as we build a basis for trust with one another. As we move to a level of honesty, we are confronted with the level of dishonesty in our current relationships. Honesty in ministry is the gift of freedom that comes when we are accepted for who we are as youth workers.

Partnership

One of the largest lessons taught in the Bible is partnership. God longs to partner with us to accomplish his purposes here on earth. That model of partnership is what we as youth workers need to strive toward.

I remember driving by a small church in our community for eleven years. My church was two blocks away, and I had never walked in the doors of this small church. One Saturday, I walked in, and the proud, young pastor greeted me and welcomed me. My heart broke as he showed me closets where kids would have their Sunday school classes and a sanctuary with a broken projector because they didn't have the money to replace the bulb. My heart broke because of the lack of desire I had previously felt to partner with a church that served just two blocks from my own.

There are ministry colleagues all around you with whom you have the ability to partner and who need you, but there are also people around you who have what *you* need. Partnership is a biblical principle that will show to the world that we are "Christ followers by our love."

Development

Ministry colleagues give you the ability to think beyond the walls of your church. There is a way to do things at your church and a grid of theology in which to operate. Many of us have become stale in our jobs and have stopped developing because we have stopped thinking. It is important to choose colleagues who push you in regards to theology, ministry practices, and life. When people who are associated with you see you developing, they in turn become passionate about their own development.

Perspective Support

Relationships with ministry colleagues will bring you a level of support that people within your church cannot bring. Whenever you are involved in a situation in the church, it becomes increasingly difficult to have a perspective that supersedes the situation. Outside ministry colleagues can help you gain a perspective that is not blemished by the realities of ministry. They are able to give you thoughts on how to lead through an issue without being attached to the issue.

There are also times when you need a person to whom to complain or even with whom to share your frustrations, and you need this person to be one who isn't attached to the relational composition of the church. In my own life, there were people who served in this role simply as listeners and were able to let me be, without having to hold it all together.

☰ **What relational need do you feel you are missing in your current relationships?**

☰ **What relational needs could you provide for some people with whom you currently have relationships?**

———

The most interesting dynamic happens as we mature in ministry and become more competent in ministry. We begin to have fewer friends and ministry relationships and become more closed in. I believe that, to remain effective in ministry, we need to desire a variety of relationships that will give us the ability to continue to lead well.

Prayer*

For this very reason, make every effort to add to your faith goodness;

and to goodness, knowledge;

and to knowledge, self-control;

and to self-control, perseverance;

and to perseverance, godliness;

and to godliness, mutual affection;

and to mutual affection, love.

For if you possess these qualities in increasing measure, they will keep you from being ineffective and unproductive in your knowledge of our Lord Jesus Christ.

---

*2 Peter 1:5-7

THIRTEEN

COMMUNITY

I am blessed with an incredibly gifted wife. She is the one who loves people and makes everyone feel like they belong. The number-one area she excels in and challenges me in is the relationships we enjoy with people who are part of the community we live in and the community around the church.

Once when I was mowing my lawn, I saw a neighbor walk across the street to come and talk with me. At first, I wasn't thrilled because I had so much work to do around the home, and I needed to go to my next appointment at the church. He asked questions that revolved around what I did for a living, and my frustration with the delay soon changed. I thought this might be my opportunity to share about my faith in Jesus. Then a powerful statement came from my neighbor: "I am not sure I could ever go to your church because your church always expects you to be there." This simple confession reframed and refocused my life moving forward.

113
*

It is easy to do the work of ministry yet fail to understand our part of God's story unfolding outside the walls of our church. One of the most important aspects of our relationship with God is to love the people who are outside the church. The reality is that this is going to involve a massive reorganization of the priorities of our lives.

I am convinced more and more that people long for relationships with us. They need to see the rhythm of life as we live it. There is no way we can develop relationships with people in our community without investing time in the communities we are part of. Not only does it involve a change in our calendars; it also involves sacrificing some of our personal resources to live out the mission of God with the people in our communities.

It is interesting that many churches are placed in or near residential communities. God didn't place the collection of churches outside the community in a standardized church row. God placed us in communities so we as a church could reach out to those individuals who view the crosses on our buildings as signs of hope.

The church has an enormous amount of resources at its disposal. We have the ability to impact communities simply by learning how to share our resources. They need volunteers who will care about what is important to their community. As we learn to care for the community near the church, it is important to come ready to listen rather than prescribe what we think they need.

≡ Whom do you have relationships with in your community currently?

≡ What do you need to change to reorder your life and your family's life so you can invest more time in your community?

≡ What relationships do you have with people in the community around the church?

≡ What are the needs of the community around the church?

———

There are many benefits that come to us personally as we invest time developing relationships with our community. These relationships allow us to be agents of restoration to a world longing for hope.

We are called to be ambassadors of the message of Christ, and this will involve us stepping outside the boundaries of the church walls.

Building relationships with spiritually searching people is not just for those who have the spiritual gift of evangelism but is a requirement for all of us. We are God's representatives on earth, and it is our responsibility to share the message of hope to this world.

It is easy to become isolated within the walls of the church, where we are separate from the concerns and issues of the world. Jesus had the ability to minister to people right where they were because he walked among them. The more involved we become with others outside the church community, the more broken we become for the world. We learn how to be advocates for those who are marginalized by the world, and our heart begins to break for those who have no voice.

It is important for us not to become so separate from the world that we lose the ability to relate to others and meet them right where they are. God calls us to come alongside the broken, the blind, those in bondage, and the least of them, and this only happens if we have a perspective that is not solely focused on the needs within our church.

Unfortunately, there are fewer and fewer people committing to be the ambassadors of Christ to a world that has little hope. As youth workers, when we commit to a life that involves others, we motivate others through our actions, not just words. So often, we try to teach through our words and not our actions. Students long to see their leaders leading.

The world longs to see the hope that is found in a Savior. As youth workers, we need to reorder the priorities of our lives to raise the value of living and breathing among a world of people who need to see the hands and feet of Jesus in practical and compelling ways.

As we invest in relationships outside of the church, we get to understand the heart of God in a deeper way. Paul reminds us in Philemon 6 of this truth. "I pray that you may be active in the sharing of your faith so that you can have a full understanding of every good thing you have in Christ."

May we not build our youth ministries void of living out the message of Christ in the communities we are a part of. The greatest contribution a youth ministry can make is to be actively involved in the community and truly bringing the kingdom of God to earth.

115
*

Prayer*

In peace, we pray to God, saying, "Lord, hear our prayer."

For the universal church, without regard to our arguments and dissent, that all may work together for the betterment of your heavenly kingdom, with right teaching, love, and community. We pray to you, O God.

Lord, hear our prayer.

For our minsters and priests, counselors, rabbis, and pastors, bishops and imams. For monastics and contemplatives, for nuns, brethren, and any who go forth to minister in your name. We pray to you, O God.

Lord, hear our prayer.

For those who strive to protect us day after day. For those who choose to give themselves to you, we pray to you, O God.

Lord, hear our prayer.

For the right use of nature all around us, for our bodies and our health, that we may be pleasing temples to your great spirit. For our earth, which is a cathedral to your love, we pray to you, O God.

Lord, hear our prayer.

For pride; for our daily work to be part of your greater family, that we may work gallantly, upholding all members of our community, never feeling ourselves less than our neighbors for who we are, how we look, or who we love; we pray to you, O God.

Lord, hear our prayer.

For those who are in despair and looking for light in their lives, we pray to you, O God.

Lord, hear our prayer.

For those who have been turned away at the doors of the church. For those removed from schools, colleges, and universities. For those forced to move from their neighborhoods or wrongly imprisoned or hospitalized. For those who must pray to you only in the secret places of their heart, we pray to you, O God.

Lord, hear our prayer.

For those who are bullied by others falsely stronger, for those who are neglected or abused, and beaten in mind, body, and spirit, we pray to you, O God.

Lord, hear our prayer.

For those who are working to reduce social and economic inequality and to make the earth a better place for all, we pray to you, O God.

Lord, hear our prayer.

For those who have so long worked in the valley of the shadow of HIV/AIDS, giving comfort where often there is none, that we may learn to take care of the living in the same exquisite way they care for the dying, we pray to you, O God.

Lord, hear our prayer.

For our community leaders and community organizations; for our schools and educational programs ; that without malice, division, or contention, they will strive to encourage our people, promote equality and justice, and pursue peace, we pray to you, O God.

Lord, hear our prayer.

For our children; for our natural children, our adoptive families, and those placed in our care, that we may lead each life toward its own direction, protect and defend their rights as human beings, and work together as a community to help each child reach their full potential. We pray to you, O God.

Lord, hear our prayer.

For our families; for those of our blood relation and those who migrate in and out of our extended families, that all will be welcome and nurtured in whatever way you see fit, reminding us always that we are not meant to live alone. We pray to you, O God.

Lord, hear our prayer.

For families going through difficult times, for parents and their children, we pray to you, O God.

Lord, hear our prayer.

For all Christians, that we may be open to your Word in our lives, we pray to you, O God.

Lord, hear our prayer.

For seekers; for those who seek to listen to your Word and put it into practice, we pray to you, O God.

Lord, hear our prayer.

Almighty God, to whom our needs are known before we ask, help us to seek only what accords with your will; and those good things which we dare not, or in our blindness cannot ask, grant us, for the sake of your Son, Jesus Christ, our Lord.

Sacred Pauses, "The Prayers of the People"

CHALLENGE

Relationships are incredibly complex and involve patience and hard work. It can be easy to say we are simply not relational, but the majority of a youth minister's life is about the ability he or she has to lead people and be led in return.

The ability to manage the different relationships you will face both inside and outside the church will be a challenging juggling act for you. You will be faced with people who long for relationship and with others who will frustrate you as you try to build relationships with them. Remember to persevere and value people for the way in which God has created them.

Many of the relationships you develop will lead to lifelong memories of people who stepped into the gap with you or people who valued your contribution to their lives. These people will make up the art of your life—a collection of images, stories, and memories that define who you are. At the end of the day, ministry is all about relationships and helping one another be everything God has created us to be.

My desire is for you to learn how to capitalize on the relationships God has blessed you with. For me, writing this book has brought so many memories. I have enjoyed being reminded of all the people and blessings—whether difficult or effortless relationships—who have crossed my path.

There are three groups of people who will come across the pages of your life on a regular basis. Pull out your calendar right now and take a look at it as you read along. Our calendars say a lot about who we are, where we spend our money, and what relationships fill up our time.

Draining Relationships

In ministry, people who need extra grace will always find you. However, God will never give you more than what you can handle. These people are some of the main reasons your ministry exists, so try not to view them as burdens in your ministry.

That being said, the draining people in your life need to have clearly set boundaries. Make sure to have a set amount of time you will give them each week, and do not let them dictate your schedule. If you allow draining people to fill up your calendar, you could end up depleting your relational tank, leaving you with nothing to contribute to others. Jesus is the perfect example of the boundaries we need to learn to implement. He knew where he was headed, and he did heal and minister as he went, but he did not lose focus.

Neutral Relationships

In our weekly routines, so much time is spent with neutral people. These types of people dominate our calendars and neither contribute significantly to nor take away from our lives. This is the vacuum of life in regard to relationships.

Neutral relationships are usually the ones that fill our calendars up with meetings and other routine obligations. Relationships are built, but they are focused on goals and the ability to use each other to complete defined tasks. Neutral relationships are neither a benefit nor an immediate hindrance. However, if not monitored, they can cause your relational tank to deplete at a slower pace until you eventually have nothing left.

Refueling Relationships

We often tend to think of the need we have for meaningful relationships last. Our calendars are full of relationships in which we must give of ourselves, but we lack a large number of relationships that refuel us. These relationships speak into who we are and give us the strength to work through the struggles that come into our weekly routines.

When we fill up our calendars, we need to set times aside for these kinds of relationships. A refueling relationship is a relationship that leaves us with smiles on our faces, and we feel ready to take on the challenges of the day. These relationships are not necessarily dependent on the quantity of time but rather the quality of the time spent. They are relationships we must proactively put into our calendars. Think through who in your life refuels you on a regular basis.

———

Ministry is a difficult job that involves a commodity that can't be controlled: people. People have the ability to bring you joy as well as pain. As we deal with people, we open ourselves up to pain, rejection, and frustration, but we also open ourselves up to joy, redemption, and restoration. You and I have been given the opportunity to be Jesus to a world that needs to see love and hope and a future.

Many verses in the Bible talk about honor. We are told to honor our parents and those who have been given authority in the world. In the New Testament, we are told to honor our spiritual leaders.

Today, as you read this, I want to honor you.

> I honor you for the commitment you make to serve God and students.
> I honor you for the sacrifices you make financially to serve God and students.
> I honor you for the sacrifices your family makes to allow you to serve God.
> I honor you for the choices you make every day to point people toward Jesus.
> I honor you because you will be one of the individuals who helps my daughters see that living a Christ-honoring life is the best choice they can make.
> I honor you because you are my family's pastor.

The road in youth ministry is never straight or easy. There are more ups and downs than a roller coaster at an amusement park. But many of the relationships you create in youth ministry can last a lifetime. Youth ministry needs to recapture the lost art of cultivating deep relationships simply by learning to love each other.

May you find the great pleasure of being a relational connector of people. May you find satisfaction in helping people feel like they belong. May you find joy in being Jesus with skin on.

Prayer*

I am no longer my own but yours.

Put me to what you will.

Put me to doing, put me to suffering.

Let me be employed for you or laid aside for you, exalted for you or brought low for you.

Let me be full or let me be empty.

Let me have all things or let me have nothing.

I freely and wholeheartedly yield all things to your disposal.

And now, glorious and blessed Father, Son, and Holy Spirit, you are mine, and I am yours.

So be it.

And the covenant now made on earth, let it be ratified in heaven.

---

*John Wesley

AFTERWORD

It is 11:29 p.m. on Saturday night of the Southern Gospel Weekend. I have been living in Room #1 of Spruce Lodge on the youth side with my family for almost eight weeks. My home this summer has been Camp Harmattan, a youth camp in the beautiful foothills of southern Alberta.

It has been a summer I didn't exactly plan. I had grand dreams to capitalize on the lazy days of summer in my backyard. Instead, I have had to count on a friend to mow my lawn. I have had to rely on others to cook my meals for me each day. The camp's summer staff has lent a hand when we didn't have enough volunteers or staff to cover all the shifts or when more people showed up than what we expected. I have had to rely on a group of people to accomplish something bigger than what we could even imagine by ourselves. It has been a summer of learning for me in the midst of turning a camp back to being sustainable and relevant.

This book took many months to get all the words to nicely fit on the pages. As I spent the last year writing this book, the panoramic view of past and present relationships (some good and some more challenging) flooded the movie screen of my mind. The months writing these chapters, in some ways, were like looking back at a yearbook and remembering certain places and situations that made me into who I am today.

The interesting thing in life is that we always tend to remember the past more fondly than it really was. It might be that time heals the pain from yesteryear or that another year older causes your perception of reality to change. God taught me a very important lesson this weekend about relationships, and it had nothing to do with the many lessons I had already covered in the writing of this book.

It started when I looked at a couple who have given up almost their entire summer to chip in and help out at the camp with whatever and whenever. It continued when I saw a group of young adults who could earn way more money in a different setting but chose to love on kids and, with God's help, spiritually transform these children's lives. It continued when I walked by the trailer of an old friend who told me that God used me in her life to effect change and that she missed me. It went on and on and on and almost became something that bombarded me by the end of the day. All these vignettes of people God has brought into my life to help me in the call God has placed on my life.

The lesson is simply this: To really have authentic relationships, you have to learn to become a great receiver.

Often in ministry relationships, we are the people who give and give and give. It becomes a drug that we live on as we rush around giving 'til there is nothing left to give. We enjoy being needed, and we love the aspect of caring for others.

I have come to understand that the majority of us—including myself—are terrible receivers. We just don't like being on the receiving end and work hard in relationships to not let that happen. Think about these places where we have a hard time receiving.

We struggle hearing praise from others about what they see in us. We struggle being cared for because we believe that we have to make it by ourselves. We struggle when others want to truly help us because we believe that we will be a burden to them. We struggle. We struggle. We struggle.

I have tried my best in the pages of this book to present a youth worker's guide to establishing healthy relationships. We have explored various relationships a youth pastor must navigate both inside and outside the church walls. The starting point was with God, who is the author and perfecter of our faith.

All of these concepts are great and will hopefully help you find an element of success in the relationships you maintain. You can go through ministry and life creating relationships that are fruitful and lasting, but they will all be missing something. That is the hardest thing as we pursue ministry friendships.

As our time together draws to an end, I leave this relationship with you from the thoughts I have scribbled down on a few pages. The concept that keeps rolling in my head is simply that you (and I) need to learn how to receive in relationships if we ever want to move beyond them being simply surface relationships.

Maybe, it is difficult to receive because many of us hold leadership positions that demand us to be in charge or to take charge. We believe that if we are in a position of receiving, then we are in a weaker and more soft leadership posture. I think (no, I am actually sure) that the success of a youth worker or of any Christian leader is in his or her ability to receive.

Each one of us hits a plateau in our relationships because they are only one dimensional. We become the only ones who give, and that instantly stunts the growth of our relationships. When Jesus says in Matthew 7:7, "Ask and it will be given to you, seek and you will find, knock and the door will be opened to you," I believe he is giving us a model for what a healthy relationship should look like. Jesus proclaims this as a model for our relationship with the Father but also our relationships here on earth.

≡ When was the last time you asked for something in a relationship? Do not just think of the extraordinary requests but something of everyday concern.

≡ When was the last time you sought out something in a relationship? It is easy for us to convince ourselves to manage everything here on earth because that is what we are supposed to do, but there are times when we are called to seek.

≡ When was the last time you knocked on a door, even though you knew you would be a disturbance or possibly a burden to that person?

———

Simply think through these points of evaluation for your own life moving forward in your different relationships.

≣ **How are you doing on those three things with God? This easily shows the depth of your relationship with God.**

≣ **How are you doing on those three things with your family? This easily shows the depth of your relationship with your family.**

≣ **How are you doing on those three things with your staff or ministry team? If you want to be a good team, you have to work toward that.**

≣ **How are you doing with those three things with your coworkers or neighbors or ministry partners?**

———

The cost of deep relationships in ministry is tough and involves a deep level of sacrifice on the part of ministry workers. The sacrifice involves authenticity in relationships and the ability to receive from people we don't feel should be giving to us. We have made the role of the pastor or ministry leader untouchable and without flaw. I believe people long for us to be real, and realness comes from a willingness to receive.

Read This Prayer from Jesus for Us*

My prayer is not for them alone. I pray also for those who will believe in me through their message, that all of them may be one, Father, just as you are in me and I am in you. May they also be in us so that the world may believe that you have sent me. I have given them the glory that you gave me, that they may be one as we are one—I in them and you in me—so that they may be brought to complete unity. Then the world will know that you sent me and have loved them even as you have loved me. Father, I want those you have given me to be with me where I am, and to see my glory, the glory you have given me because you loved me before the creation of the world. Righteous Father, though the world does not know you, I know you, and they know that you have sent me. I have made you known to them, and will continue to make you known in order that the love you have for me may be in them and that I myself may be in them.

And this is my prayer for you too.
May you be good receivers and good givers of hope!

127
*

---

*John 17:20-26

bare foot
MINISTRIES®

Helping youth workers guide students into spiritual formation for the mission of God.

———

Barefoot is devoted to providing

churches around the world with

practical, relevant, inspiring, and

affordable resources to help

youth and young adults

find and follow Jesus.

Don't hesitate to contact us if we

can help you or your faith community

with our resources as you seek

to guide students into spiritual

formation for the

mission of God!

———

www.BarefootMinistries.com